RIDGE RUNNER

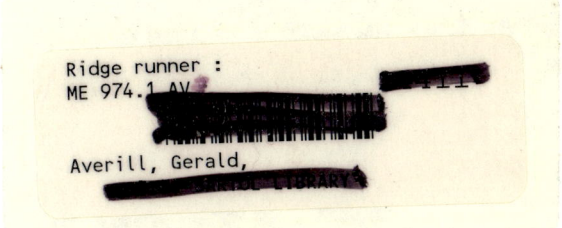

974.1

GERALD AVERILL

RIDGE RUNNER

The Story of a Maine Woodsman

Illustrated by Peter Stanziale

The Thorndike Press

Library of Congress Cataloging in Publication Data

Averill, Gerald, 1896-
  Ridge runner.

  Autobiography.
  Reprint of the ed. published by Lippincott,
Philadelphia.
  1. Averill, Gerald, 1896- 2. Maine—Description and
travel. 3. Game Wardens—Maine—Biography.
I. Title.
SK354.A93A37   1979   974.1'04'0924(B)   79-14339
ISBN 0-89621-031-6
ISBN 0-89621-030-8 pbk.

Copyright renewed 1976 in the name of Edith
Averill, Reprinted by The Thorndike Press by
arrangement with Gerald P. Averill.

INTRODUCTION

My father never saw a printed, bound, copy of *Ridge Runner*. He saw the galley proofs, revised them and rewrote them, at the direction of the publisher...but that was as close as he came. It would have brought him tremendous satisfaction, could he have seen the finished product, but that was not to be. He died of cancer in 1946. *Ridge Runner* was published in 1948.

I was away in the Pacific, fighting or preparing to fight the Marine Corps battles of World War II, during the period when *Ridge Runner* was written. I too, saw the galley proofs, when I was home on leave in October and November of 1946. For the short time we had together, I shared my father's thoughts, his sense of accomplishment at having completed the book, and in the happiness engendered by the anticipation of that momentous occasion...the day when the first run of books would commence. Early in November I left Maine for Camp Pendleton, California. A few days after my arrival there, he was dead.

My father loved the State of Maine...all of it...but most of all the wilderness areas. He was at his best in the woodlands, along the trout streams...on the waters of the lakes and rivers. He was totally at peace with himself and with mankind, in those places...his only real contentment, there. As a child I went with him. He taught me to shoot, to hunt and fish...to enjoy the sights, the sounds, the smells of the forest. On those forays we might not speak for hours on end, pausing in movement only when his sharp eyes would perceive some animal, bird or plant, with which he wanted to acquaint me. He was attuned to

Nature...moving with it, living with it, savoring all its aspects, feeling its mysteries stir him deep inside.

All of the places about which my father wrote in *Ridge Runner* I have visited..sometimes in his company...sometimes alone. When my children were young, they moved along the same trails that I had traversed with my father. When the book was first published, it soon became apparent that a great number of other people had also been to those places, or to places that resembled them...for the book had a truly phenomenal run for one of its particular type and size. This winter, when Mr. Phillips Treleaven of *The Thorndike Press* wrote to me suggesting that the book be reprinted, I was delighted, for I am sure that there remain many people in the State of Maine, who will enjoy the recounting of old legends and the tales of woods lore that appear on the pages of *Ridge Runner*. I was *told* most of those stories before my father ever set out to write them down, and now, when I open that little book, I find that the written words retain all of the flavor, the tang, the palatability, of those words spoken to me so long ago.

My only regret is that my father could not know of this second printing. It is my opinion that it would have pleased him even more than the first...for to realize that one's work is still appreciated, still sought after over the years, is surely an accolade of infinite substance.

    Gerald P. Averill
    Lientenant Colonel U.S. Marine Corps (Ret)
    24 February, 1979

CHAPTER I

My grandfather placed a stick of cordwood carefully upon the saw-horse and sat down upon it. His motions were slow and deliberate, as he removed his ragged mittens and prepared to fill his pipe. The ritual of filling and lighting that pipe was something not to be undertaken lightly, or in haste. First came the pipe—one of those elaborate creations with a filigree of near-gold around the rim of the bowl, an amber mouthpiece stained a rich, dark brown from use, and more tarnished gold where the mouthpiece entered the stem. The pipe was always carried in a case. A wooden case covered with thin leather and lined with blue satin. One pushed a little button under the place where the bowl fitted and the case opened on tiny brass hinges. My grandfather closed the case which snapped shut and locked itself by some mysterious means. The pipe went into the right side of his mouth where two of his remaining teeth could hold it in a position of doubtful security. The case went back into the pocket from whence it came and the same hand appeared magically with a knife.

The knife was opened—an act which required the use of both hands. Since it was a two-blader, the smaller was reserved entirely for the purpose of cutting tobacco, for it was a well-known fact that plug tobacco drew the temper from the steel and ruined it for whittling purposes. The pipe was removed from his mouth, grasped between the thumb and first finger of the left hand, and the bowl energetically reamed of carbon and residue which was deposited in the left palm to add strength and flavor to the new charge. The knife took the place of the pipe in his left hand while my grandfather returned the pipe to his mouth and blew strongly through the stem. More often than not it would be plugged tight, but this time, after a gurgle of protest, it partially cleared.

Now, while the pipe seemed to quiver with anticipation in my grandfather's beard, his right hand groped deep in a rear pocket and emerged with a new cut of Sickle Plug which took the place of the knife between the thumb and index finger of the left hand. It was grasped firmly by the entire length of the thumb and the first two fingers in such a way as to leave the cupped palm, still holding the scrapings of the bowl, in a position to receive the shavings from the plug. My grandfather never looked at his tobacco while he was cutting it. His eyes would stray aloft to examine the sky, linger over the face of the town clock, or stare fixedly up the village street while he slowly pinched off bits of tobacco between his thumb and the knife blade and deposited them with the charred remains of the previous filling.

I was always fascinated by the next move, for by some feat of magic, when the exact amount of tobacco was cut, the knife, a second before firmly grasped by his right hand, suddenly popped through the first and second finger to be held there blade out. Then, still holding the plug in his left, he began with a slow rotary motion to grind the tobacco between his palms. When the coarse mixture was reduced to a point where there was a possibility of its burning, the knife was closed, returned to its proper pocket, the tobacco disappeared, and only then did my grandfather allow himself to survey the work of his hands. The pipe, which by this time was visibly drooling in anticipation, was removed from his beard and the contents of his palm carefully worked into its bowl and tamped there solidly by a calloused thumb. There was never too much tobacco, or too little. The bowl was always filled to its utmost capacity, and yet there was never a crumb wasted.

All this was in preparation for the real ceremony—that of obtaining fire and applying it to the tobacco. Next, from an inner pocket came a brass match box always well filled with Portland Star matches. These were the forerunner of the common kitchen match and were very popular with farmers and woodsmen long after a better product appeared on the market, for the simple reason that they could be water-soaked and still be serviceable when dried. These matches came in sheets or cards, as they were called. The top of the card was cut in and serrated like the top of a picket fence and dipped in an odorous composition in which sulphur predominated. When a match was wanted, it was broken off the card, and if a suitable surface could be found to create friction, after some delay, considerable fuming and spluttering, a feeble flame would result.

My grandfather broke off a match and scratched it carefully on the bottom of the box which was roughened for that very purpose. He was lucky, as well as skillful, for at the very first attempt a tiny blue glow appeared, followed by sulphurous fumes. Holding the match in his cupped palms and shielding it from the wind, he waited for the second stage of combustion when the blue would give place to yellow flame. It was necessary at this time to keep the match a respectable distance from his face, for the reek of burning sulphur if taken into the throat and nostrils would have about the same effect as a kick in the stomach. Finally, after careful nursing, a very feeble flame appeared and the match was gingerly applied to the pipe bowl. My grandfather puffed. His cheeks caved in with the energy of his puffings and gradually a thin wisp of smoke emerged from his beard. The tobacco grew red—it became a bright coal. The pipe gurgled joyfully and my grandfather spat copiously. He was ready to talk.

It was early in the spring, the ice had just left our river after a thrilling period of indecision during which it had carried away one bridge in the village and threatened to do away with the other. For a day and a night it had piled high against the piers of the Lower Bridge and thrown great cakes where river ice had never been seen before. Half the village had been flooded and the schoolhouse had been one of the first buildings to suffer. Its basement and ground floor had been thoroughly innundated, and the basement, where the year's supply of fuel was stored, was still full of water.

It was truly a time of great rejoicing, for the school was closed and nobody knew when it could be opened again. It had been a very satisfactory disaster. There had been much scurrying about, chopping of ice and finally the boom of blasting powder that had released the flood and saved the bridge. There was still much to be seen and more to be talked about, but owing to some digression from the paths of righteousness, I found myself segregated from my fellows, in a state of limited confinement. I was forbidden to leave home unless upon a necessary errand. The house, the woodshed and the immediate area surrounding the buildings were the walls of my prison, and within these barren confines I had languished for two whole days, until hearing of my sad plight my grandfather had put forth an urgent plea for help at his woodpile, thus releasing me from sheer boredom to a period of hard labor. I was not much taller than the axe and handle together, but I had labored right manfully swinging the heavy four-pound axe between long periods of rest and one-sided conversation. My grandfather was a very reasonable man. He believed that chewing tobacco was good for a toothache and, while working with him, I always had quite a lot of trouble with my teeth.

The sun had shone brightly on that morning of my deliverance, but now, later in the day, the wind was from the south, blowing strongly and driving a wide bank of fog before it. The smell of salt water, flats mud and the great marshes of the South Branch came in with the fog. It was the first heavy odor of early spring and open water, and the air tasted good. My grandfather took his pipe from his mouth and raised his face to the sky. From high above us through the thickening mist came the thin, lonesome clamor of wild geese. They went over us toward the Penobscot and there seemed to be a note of alarm in their faint trumpetings. I held my breath and listened, and in a few moments we heard them come back over us a little to the north.

My grandfather had a habit of blinking, and now he puffed hard on his pipe and opened and shut his eyes rapidly in time with his puffing.

"H'm," he said softly. "H'm."

I sat there on the chopping block, waiting impatiently, with my mouth wide open. I knew he was going to say something important and it had to be about the geese. It seemed as if I waited hours and then, when I was almost ready to burst, because of the dampness, the poor burning qualities of the tobacco, or an act of Providence, his pipe went out.

My grandfather was not a constant smoker. There was a proper time for the use of tobacco, and burning it was a serious business. So when, after a decent interval of peace, during which a sufficient quantity of that acrid, saliva-provoking effluvium had been drawn into his mouth and blown out, his pipe went out. That was the end of it until a rest from labor or the termination of a meal provided another opportunity for indulgence.

And so, the pipe with its reeking contents was returned to its case, my grandfather wiped his mouth with a large bandanna figured in blue and white, cleared his throat and gave me all his attention.

"Them geese," he observed positively, "is lost."

Now the statement that a flock of wild geese could get lost was certainly debatable, but coming from my grandfather, it was nothing less than confounding. For at least four long years and over two hundred interminable sessions of Sunday school, the fact had been hammered into my reluctant brain that fowls of the air lived and moved and had their being under a special divine patronage. What about that sparrow? If God could keep a check on the movements of one small bird, it did not seem reasonable that a whole flock of birds the size of geese would be allowed to spend the remainder of their lives blundering around in the fog.

It would never have done for me to put my expression of doubt into words, for in those days an opinion voiced in opposition to a statement from an older person might be construed as "talking back," a practice much frowned upon among the best people and usually followed by unpleasant results.

My face must have shown some evidence of perplexity, for my grandfather hastened to explain that the geese were not going to stay lost, that they were just temporarily bewildered by the fog.

"Them geese," he declared, "is lookin' for open water. Soon as they get over the mountain and over the main river, they'll drop down there and maybe stay two, three days. I bet a red apple that tomorrow mornin' at the peak o' the tide them geese will be into Grant's Cove. I bet a *big* red apple that if we was to be there, we could get us one an' maybe two."

This was too much! Here was I, temporarily released from durance vile to serve out a short sentence at hard labor, asked to participate in my first goose hunt. I slid from the chopping block, folded my arms upon it, buried my face and wept. My grief was sincere though muffled. There were times when punishment could make it audible for miles—if the wind was right—but this was too deep to be noisy. It really hurt.

I don't think my grandfather ever intended to go after those geese. In the beginning he was merely making conversation, but the sight and sound of my weeping and the knowledge of what caused it roused him to action. He was a very quiet man, but also a very determined one.

He pried me loose from the block and attempted to dry my tears. "Hey, let up," he whispered. "The neighbors'll think I'm butcherin' a hog. What'd you do to get into trouble anyway?"

I managed between hiccups to tell him that I thought it was because I had torn my pants.

"So," said my grandfather softly. "So you tore your pants. Well, I'll be damned! I'll be everlastingly *good goddamned!* Most time for your father to be home from work, an' I'll see him about this."

My father was a stern man who tried to be just. He worked nine hours a day hewing at great slabs of Mount Waldo granite and seemed to find little in life to be joyful about. I suppose he loved me as much as any father could love such an unattractive little runt as I was at that time, but his goings gave me a temporary sense of freedom and relief, while his comings were looked forward to with the dread of a chicken-hearted criminal about to be brought before the bar of justice. My mother usually had a list of my misdemeanors for him to review every night, and I suspect that most of the time he was too tired to do any more than impose sentence without hearing my poor defense. My grandfather sometimes appeared for me, but often did more harm than good, especially when pleading before my mother. I think she was just a little ashamed of her father and I believe my grandfather knew it.

We lived in a house with running water in the sink and hardwood floors downstairs—one of the very few houses in the village equipped with such modern conveniences—and my mother was one of those housewives, who, though ailing a great part of the time, "worked her fingers to the bone" and complained constantly of her hard lot. My grandfather was very uneasy when at our house. There was no place to spit and he was known as a very free spitter.

My father had little contact with my mother's blood relatives, but I know that he liked my grandfather and respected certain qualities in him that might not have been evident to the opposite sex. Anyway, when they met, it was on grounds of mutual respect and there was never any suspicion of unpleasantness between them.

I do not know what passed between them that afternoon, but my grandfather came home in a very good humor. He was so jovial in fact that my grandmother suspected a hidden bottle and cast dark glances in his direction.

"Well," he chuckled, "now that everything is fixed up, we got just about enough daylight left to go up in the shed chamber and ram a couple of goose charges into the old Greener Gun."

The shed chamber was my grandfather's personal refuge. His greatest treasures were kept there, and although I was allowed access at all times, I never entered it without wondering what new source of pleasure and amusement I might next discover. Before the eye could grasp the orderly profusion of various materials offering unlimited opportunity for play or mischief, the nose was assailed by the most provocative and seductive accumulation of smells ever allowed to concentrate under one small roof.

Ridge Runner 17

The combined odors of beeswax, tar, cedar, linseed oil, paint, and turpentine struggled mightily to overcome the ripeness of several fish kegs in which my grandfather salted down mackerel. This titillating conglomeration of rugged perfumes was strongly permeated by the odor of hens, from the floor below, especially on a damp day.

There was unlimited wood for whittling, festoons of rope and codline, balls of carefully saved string, and a great sea chest filled with tools enough to stock a carpenter shop. In addition to lumps of strong-smelling beeswax there was half a keg of tar, and either substance was a very good substitute for chewing gum even if it did cause the tongue and mouth some irritation.

All this was mine. All except the Greener Gun which was hung from two of the rafters in loops of harness leather, supposedly well out of my reach. The gun, or the "Greener Gun," as my grandfather always called it, was a most fearsome piece of ordnance. It was a double-barreled muzzle-loader weighing close to twelve pounds and must have been about ten bore. Its barrels were thirty-four inches long and both of them had about six inches of shallow rifling at the muzzle—a feature of English origin. (As I learned later a shotgun thus bored was called a Paradox.) My grandfather set great store by this almost unknown innovation and claimed it caused the gun to shoot much farther and harder than an ordinary smooth-bore. There was a great powder horn, scraped so thin that one could see its contents almost as plainly as if viewed through glass, and a leather shot pouch that was slung over the opposite shoulder from the powder horn. The small metal box of percussion caps was carried where it could be gotten at quickly—usually in the handiest coat pocket.

The contents of the shot pouch are worthy of note. My grandfather believed that the larger sizes of shot would kill at a greater distance than the smaller pellets and that they should be available at all times. Knowing, too, that the smaller shot gave closer patterns and covered an area more completely, he refused to be without any advantage that they might offer. The Greener Gun, being what it was, was not capable of accepting any variety of loads without going through a long and tedious process of drawing charges and reloading from the muzzle, so my grandfather solved all loading problems by filling the pouch with a mixture of various shot sizes ranging from 00 Buck down to number twelve or "mustard seed." A generous helping of this mixture ahead of about four drams of black powder invariably created a vast disturbance, and according to my grandfather, resulted in sure death to anything within a range of a hundred yards.

Since the Greener Gun had not been fired for months, loading it was an operation requiring a certain amount of preparatory investigation. First, both barrels had to be carefully probed with a rod equipped with a corkscrew sort of attachment called a "worm." This was for the purpose of locating and removing any foreign substance, or a forgotten charge from some previous loading. A thin piece of wire thrust into the nipples made sure of a clean opening from the cap to the powder, and then my grandfather poured the glistening grains of black powder from the horn into an empty ten gauge brass shell which was used as a measure. On this occasion he dumped the usual stiff charge into the barrels and then, muttering something about geese being tough, he added more powder direct from the horn. This was followed by a wad of well-fluffed oakum which was rammed down upon the powder charge until the ramrod, bringing up against it, sounded as though it were hitting a solid block of wood. I don't know how many ounces of shot went into those old barrels, but there must have been a good half-handful in each load, held down by a top wad of at least a solid inch of hard-packed oakum. The ramrod thumped and thumped until at last it would spring nearly clear of the barrel. My grandfather wiped the breech and stock with an oily rag. The stock was of dark, satiny wood, very pleasant to the touch, and on its right side near the middle was a small silver plate upon which was engraved in flowery letters, "Geo H. Walker."

That was my grandfather's name.

My grandfather's house was in some ways like him—small and snug and set solidly upon good foundations. Most of the living was done in the kitchen which was the largest and warmest room in the house. It was always overheated and full of good homey smells, especially during the cooler months when the whole house was hermetically sealed against damp or frost.

My grandmother, an Irish lady of uncertain temper and comfortable girth, was vastly contemptuous of New England standards of housekeeping. As long as there was warmth and food in abundance, she was satisfied, and considered poking in corners and picking out cracks a sad waste of time and energy. My grandfather was one of the few completely fearless men I have ever known, but when my grandmother, for some reason known only to herself, engaged in one of her frequent "slatting spells," he would retire to his corner behind the stove until the bang of skillets and stove lids quieted down. Nobody knew why or when she would be suddenly overtaken by one of these black rages, for in this respect she was, as my grandfather put it, "entirely unpredictable.' Judged by the standards of my mother and associates, my grandmother was a very poor cook and the results of her culinary efforts were apt to be as uncertain as her temper.

My mother's biscuits were small, light and entirely perfect. They could furnish just two delicious bites to a hungry boy and there were never enough of them. My grandmother's were nearly as big around as a saucer and they would stay stubbornly in the pan refusing to rise up and compete with perfection. They had flavor and substance and a tough yet absorbent quality that was matchless in its ability to sop up bean juice, gravy, the yolks of fried eggs, or any other semi-liquids that could not be handled with ordinary table tools. My mother's biscuits were prone to crumble, but my grandmother's never did. They had a certain elastic composition that made them practically indestructible.

A great part of the food that appeared on my grandfather's table was seasonal. There would be fresh pork or beef during the fall and early winter, veal in the early spring; and when the spring run began in the rivers, smelts, alewives and Penobscot River salmon. The butcher's canvas-covered wagon came once a week during the warm months, but the meat seemed always slightly tainted. You could smell its rankness while it was cooking. Butter was always half melted and strong smelling and fresh milk would often sour overnight, so I refused both, thus creating a constant source of bickering and scolding and minor punishments at home. However, my grandfather used condensed milk, which I was very fond of, and he was entirely indifferent whether I ate butter or not.

There were two dishes served by my grandmother that I have never seen surpassed or equalled. Her baked beans and rabbit stew. Maine is famous for the quality of its baked beans and I have eaten them prepared by some of the most famous woods cooks and hotel chefs of my time. I have gorged on them from freshly opened bean holes in the big timber and on the log drives and sampled freely from the ovens in immaculate farm kitchens, but I have never seen or tasted any that equalled the satisfying richness of the homegrown yellow-eyes and cranberries that came from my grandmother's blackened earthen bean pot.

At home we had beans Saturday night for supper. We had them again Sunday morning for breakfast, warmed up in a frying pan, and that was the end of them until another Saturday. They were good beans and probably, from a strictly nutritional standpoint, the best in the village, but they were invariably of the California pea variety and lacking in flavor. My mother considered "big beans" to be somewhat plebeian and vulgar and would not use them, even though my grandfather would have gladly given us all we needed.

At my grandfather's house there were beans every day. My grandmother must have used two pots, for I remember there was always one nearly full on the back of the stove, just at the right temperature for eating, and there was almost always an empty pot soaking in the sink in the buttery. Being concerned only with the finished product, I never watched her prepare them for the oven, but knowing her careless methods of cookery, I am sure she employed no secret formula unless it had to do with the big onion always found in the bottom of the pot. It is certain that this onion contributed greatly to the fragrance emanating from a freshly opened pot of my grandmother's beans, but it can hardly account for the superb baking that left each bean smooth, glistening, with an entirely unbroken skin, yet soft enough to be crushed with the tongue against the roof of the mouth. And the juice! Never too thin, never watery, but thick, oily and filled with goodness from the generous piece of salt pork baked to a jelly-like consistency except for the streak of lean which was always included in my first helping—because I was "growing and needed it." Dip half a biscuit in this sustaining fluid and you had something on your bread more nourishing and flavorful than any butter ever churned.

I don't remember how the rabbit stew was made, but except for about three months of the year it appeared regularly at least once a week. There was plenty of rabbit meat in it together with onions, carrots, turnips, potatoes and a suspicion of cabbage. It had to simmer a long time before it was ready to eat, and the more it was warmed up the better it tasted. It was thick and dark and powerful and sometimes there were dumplings in it. Quite often one's teeth would grind down upon a shot, and then again there were many rabbits that went into that big iron kettle that were put there without the expenditure of powder and lead. There is no proof of this, but very often there were no shot in the rabbits and my grandfather always carried a small coil of fine copper wire when he roamed the woods.

My grandfather opened the kitchen door and said, "Mary, we have company for supper and to spend the night."

"And," I added joyfully, "tomorrow we go goose hunting."

My grandmother gave a slat and a flounce, dashed a handful of silverware upon the table, whirled and made a rush for the stove, yanked a great pan of biscuits from the oven, and rapped upon one of them with a stiff forefinger.

"Company it is!" she muttered. "And nothing in this house for a pig to eat. The black shame upon us that one should come hungry here and no decent bit to offer them."

As this was her usual reaction and greeting, my grandfather winked at me and then retreated to his chair behind the stove to remove his rubbers and larrigans while I kicked off my rubbers and hung up my outside wraps.

I washed sketchily at the sink amidst a great rattling and clashing of dishes at the table, and my grandmother interrupted her constant muttering long enough to shout, "Will ye have beans, or shall I fry some eggs?"

I made known my preference for beans and almost immediately the kitchen was filled with an odor so rich that three good whiffs of it contained as much nourishment as a bowl of thick soup.

It was now dusk and my grandmother lighted the tall

lamp and set it on the table. She served us great helpings of beans direct from the pot and shoved a plate of biscuits midway of the table within easy reach of us both. My grandfather's tea was poured into an enormous flowered moustache cup which he seldom drank from, preferring to pour from it to his saucer and drink the cooled tea from that. My grandfather always wore a full beard in the winter and sometimes he had quite a time straining his tea through it. My grandmother hardly ever ate with us. She retired to her rocker by the stove from whence she would make sudden, furious rushes to replenish our plates and renew the supply of biscuits.

My grandfather was a small man but a hearty feeder. It took some time for him to prepare his food, but once everything was arrangèd to his liking, he ate quickly and steadily with little pause for conversation. He liked strained honey on his beans and he would pour it on carefully, mix it thoroughly with his beans, pushing them this way and that, scrape them into a tall mound, pat them flat, build them up again and then when you were least expecting it, his knife would slip into the mound of beans, emerge covered with them almost its entire length and disappear into his whiskers. I mean no disrespect when I say that my grandfather was the handiest man with a bone-handled steel table knife that I have ever seen. He could eat anything with it except thin soup and his performance was entirely effortless. Once in a great while a green pea would get away from him, especially when it was late in the season and they were getting hard, but ordinarily he ate what was before him with neatness and dispatch and with no thought of impropriety.

In later years during my work in the lumber camps of the North, I saw many expert knife-men perform at table, but although they were good, they knew it and seemed to show a certain self-consciousness that was completely lacking in my grandfather's technique. Through watching him closely I attained a more than fair proficiency myself, but in practicing this achievement at home I found that my skill was little appreciated and, instead of approbation, I gained a set of bruised knuckles and was sent off to bed with my supper half eaten.

After my grandmother's third trip to the bean pot, I began to have difficulty in swallowing and finally to my everlasting shame I had to give up and actually leave half a biscuit dripping with honey upon my plate. I remember this meal and every last belly-stretching detail connected with it, because soon after my grandfather told me the story of the white shark.

He was a great story-teller and, although his vocabulary was limited to the simplest of words, he could make the things he talked of appear before your eyes and become more vivid than any painted picture. There were more famous narrators in our village, and some gifted liars, but none of them could breathe life into things long dead and make them pass before you as my grandfather could.

When my grandmother had cleared the table and stoked the stove, he filled his pipe, spread a newspaper upon the floor beside his chair, placed the tin spittoon upon the paper and settled himself for the short evening. He spat copiously and frequently while smoking, but because of his thick beard he was not very accurate.

Crammed full of biscuits and beans, I was becoming slightly drowsy but fought manfully to appear wide awake and alert because I knew that in all reason there should be more talk of geese and hunting and that if my head should nod I would be sent to bed.

My grandfather seemed uneasy. He took out his match box, selected a match, looked at it thoughtfully, laid it on the table, belched loudly and then shivered slightly. He looked at the window on his left, squirmed around and peered at the door behind him and muttered something about a draft. He groaned—somewhat feebly, to be sure—rubbed his stomach and attempted another belch that failed to sound impressive. Then, loudly and firmly: "Mary, is there any hot water?"

"There is," answered my grandmother shortly.

"My stomach seems to be a little upset," said my grandfather, pitifully. "I seem to feel a draft, and I have a pain in the small of my back. I think perhaps I'll . . ."

" 'Twill do no harm," my grandmother said. "The damp weather is bad for old bones, but take care."

So my grandfather got spryly from his chair, my grandmother brought him a heavy water glass, and taking a small lamp he opened the door to the cellar and went down the stairs. He returned with the glass a third full of amber liquid, and when he had filled it with hot water, added a little sugar and stirred it vigorously, the room was filled with the ripe odor of bourbon whiskey. He offered me a sip, but having only just recently signed the pledge at Sunday school, I reluctantly refused.

Settled comfortably in his chair again, my grandfather drank off half the contents of the tumbler, sighed gratefully and lighted his pipe. My grandmother watched him with the hint of a smile at the corners of her mouth.

" 'Tis best taken before eating," she said. " 'Twill have a hard time finding its way to your blood and bones through all that beans and bread."

"Ha," returned my grandfather jovially, "I can feel the first half already swampin' a road for the second, which will soon follow after and find easy goin'."

The kettle hummed upon the stove; there was a soft singing sound from the lamp. The smoke from my grandfather's pipe drifted across the room in thin, grey layers, dipped suddenly at the stove and then fled upward. My eyes suddenly refused to focus and my head drooped forward toward the table. Something had to be done, and that immediately. I snapped erect and spoke quickly: "Grandpa, did you ever shoot a goose?"

My grandfather jumped as though one of his bees had stung him, and the look he gave me was startled, questioning, and at the same time a little accusing.

His eyes were small, deep-set and of the clearest blue —honest far-seeing eyes that wept easily from grief or laughter. They examined me long and carefully, and then convinced that my question was not prompted by any actual doubt of his prowess, turned reflectively toward the ceiling.

"I," said my grandfather impressively, "have probably killed more geese than any man in the State of Maine. And," he added still more impressively, "with one shot, too."

He gave time for this astounding fact to sink in, puffed strongly upon his pipe, and went on:

"We was on a gunboat cruisin' off the coast of South Carolina a little earlier than this in the spring of the year, watchin' for blockade runners and every now and then workin' in toward shore to drop a few shells where it would stir up the Rebs and aggravate 'em. We ran into rough weather of a Tuesday, an' that night we anchored in this little bay about a mile offshore. It blew hard all that night, fit to blow the rivets out of a jackknife handle, an' all night long we could hear geese callin' and cryin' overhead an' all around us. We rode low in the water and warn't none of us slept much that night with the wind drivin' the hull up against the anchor chains and the waves breakin' clean over us at times, but 'long towards mornin' the tide turned, the gale slackened and we rode more easy. The seas calmed to a stiddy swell and at full daybreak she was pretty calm. You could look out to sea and tell it was still rough outside, but in where we was it had flattened out real pretty. Yes sir, it was quite a sight, that bay was, because when it was light enough to see good the whole surface of her was packed with geese. Nobody ever in this world ever saw such a mess of geese before or since and never will again.

"There they was, a solid raft of 'em, an' why they didn't fly off when they saw us, I don't know, unless it was because they was packed in so tight they couldn't fly. Well, the skipper come down to my gun deck and says to me, 'George,' he says, 'George, load that number four gun with canister and a good dose of musket balls an' lay in onto 'em. I'm sick of rotten salt beef an' weevily bread. Give 'em all the gun will stand, but don't bust her or foul the tackle.' So we opened her up, gave her a full charge of powder and another quarter, run down a charge of canister an' ten pounds of small shot on top of it, an' I laid her. I laid her high to get the benefit of the stringers from them musket balls an' touched her off. She come back into the britchin' pretty hard, but didn't jump the track or foul the riggin' an', Lord God, when the smoke cleared away, I wisht you could have seen them geese! The air was full of live ones an' the bay half full of dead ones, an' there was enough goose feathers scattered around to make a feather bed for every family in the State of Maine. We put two boats over and hauled geese until there jest wasn't room for any more aboard. We picked an' dressed geese until the sight an' smell of a goose-gut would make me gag an' we et goose for days on end. Hell, I bet I killed geese enough with that one shot to feed the whole Union navy for a week—maybe a month."

He finished the contents of his glass, smacked his lips appreciatively, and suggested tactfully that as there was a flood tide at eight in the morning and we had a long walk ahead of us, it might be well to go to bed.

This suggestion met with instant and vehement opposition. I wanted another story, preferably about hunting, but stated reasonably enough that any tale involving birds, beasts or fish would do. My grandfather saw that there was no evidence of drowsiness, so he told me the story of the white shark.

CHAPTER II

I can't remember the name of the ship my grandfather was on at the time all this happened. Most of them had female names, *Mabel, Ida, Emma,* or any of a dozen others. It might have been any of them bound for South America from New York or Boston. All seamen go into tedious details of ships' names, ports, cargoes and officers' names—details which are prone to slip the memory of a small boy. But, the shark! Let my grandfather tell of the white shark.

"Sometimes he would hang under the stern in the shade and then again you might see him on either side. All of thirty feet long he was, and a dirty white color. He would cruise out amongst the lighters taking the cargo ashore, and the black boys would shriek and gabble like a pack of monkeys. Not a lick of work could be got out of them while he was in sight. We shot at his back-fin with rifles and the cook spent half his time fishin' for him with a great hook fastened to a short length of small chain, the hook buried deep in a piece of salt beef or pork. We couldn't kill or catch him, for he would take a piece of meat quick enough if tossed to him free, but would not touch the piece with the hook into it. He worried the crew and slowed the work an' we hated him. And then one day one of the crew workin' on the winch leaned over the rail to clear a fouled line, lost his footin' an' went over the side. On the way down, he tore open his leg on a piece of stagin', an' when he hit the water, he was bleedin' bad. The shark come around from the stern, backed up, took a good look, an' then went for him. We had a line over to him with a noose into it, an' this man—Bowles was his name—had the noose over his head an' under his arms before you could spit. He was quick about it, but not quick enough. Before we could lift him clear of the water, the shark struck him high above the right knee in the thick of the leg where he had been hurt. Bowles was a big tough man an' the shark set his teeth an' shook him like a dog shakes a woodchuck, tryin' to tear his mouthful loose. I was one of those a-hold of the rope and it was a terrible thing to feel the tuggin' an' pullin' while Bowles kept up a steady, low groanin' with every breath. An' then all at once the shark give a lurch an' rolled clean over, takin' all the meat from the man's upper leg an' thigh. We brought him over the side an' he died hard, Bowles did, hard, but soon, an' I hope I never see a sight like that leg again.

"Well, the skipper was wild with rage. The captain of the lighter crews couldn't get his men to work an' two-thirds of our crew wouldn't go near the rail. Things was all at a standstill while that old dirty white hellion jest lay under the stern and licked his chops for more of the same. I thought and studied about the matter all night and next mornin' I went aft an' asked the skipper if I could have a try at gettin' rid of the critter.

"'Man,' he says, 'go ahead and do anything an' use

anything aboard jest so long as you get that thing without any risk.'

"So I went about it.

"We had some chickens an' three shoats aboard. The shoats were small, not much more'n suckin' pigs. An' there was an old cannon mounted in the forepeak—not much of a gun an' never used, only once in a while for signalin'. But there was half a dozen solid shot around eight pound in weight for her, an' I had me a scheme to give that shark the damndest bellyache since Eve et that apple.

"Jest before dark me an' Chips, the carpenter, moved his portable forge over to the port rail a little aft of midships an' laid out some gear we needed. Then we went forrard an' cabbaged onto one of the shoats. We brought him back to the rail where the forge was, an' Chips hit him a lick between the eyes with a hammer an' held him over the side whilst I cut his throat.

"The shark warn't nowhere around in sight, but soon as the blood hit the water a pilot fish swum out from under the stern, nosed into the blood an' then went back where he come from, like a streak. In about three seconds the shark shot out from under the ship, went through the patch of bloody water, whirled an' hung jest under us lookin' like Death an' the Devil. He was all excited up, backin' an' startin' an' tryin' to smell an' see in all directions to once, an' when I let go the pig an' it struck the water, there was jest one great flash an' swirl an' the shoat was gone. Warn't no nosin' around this time!

"The skipper was watchin' all this an' was mighty

curious about it all, but he had give me a free hand, so he kept aft an' stuck by his word.

"We didn't do no more that night, except a little tinkerin' that was needful, but along about two hours before daybreak me an' Chips lit up a fire in the forge an' laid out the things we needed. We had some good English coal, an' when we had her goin' good, we put that cast iron shot into the heart of the fire an' began to heat her up. That ball warn't very big, maybe three or three an' a half inches through, but she was heavy an' would take a lot of heat. We wanted her white hot if we could get her that way, so I pumped away at the bellows, while Chips tended the fire an' turned the ball.

"Well, it begun to get light an' the skipper rolled out. He come down where we was an' looked at the forge an' the shot an' me an' Chips an' at the bucket of sand an' the little canvas bag I had made an' opened up flat on the deck. It was jest a round piece of heavy canvas with a drawstring run through the edges an' it was laid out close by the bucket of wet sand. He was a stiff-necked man an' too proud to ask questions, but he stood by, sayin' nothin'.

"The ball began to get bright yeller an' Chips turned her an' then went after another shoat. We knocked it on the head, cut its throat and dreened the blood into a bucket we had ready, an' then we cut a slit in its belly an' took out most of the guts. We put them into the bucket with the blood an' set it by. We cut some slits lengthwise of the pig's body in the back an' flanks an' rove a piece of light line through 'em so that a quick pull and a square knot would close the openin' in the belly, an' laid the critter on his back.

"Things had got to the point now where we had to move quick an' sure. The shot was as hot as it ever would be, so I poured wet sand onto my sack, an' laid out the ends of the drawstring so that I could grab 'em quick an' handy. I took the bucket of blood an' guts an' dribbled it over the side, an' by the time the last of it was in the water the shark was into it, crazy wild. There was jest enough of the gurry to whet his appetite an' make him remember that fat little pig he had for supper the night before. Well, we was all ready an' Chips tonged out the ball, dropped it onto the pile of sand on my spread-out sack. I grabbed up a double handful of sand, threw it on top of the ball, yanked the drawstring tight, while Chips held open the slit in the pig's belly, an' dropped the sack in. Chips gave a smart haul on the line around the pig, knotted her quick an' over the side she went. Boy, that was a neat job of work—not even a wisp of smoke showed!

"Everything went jest like we planned. When that pig hit the water, the shark went for it like a pickerel for a minner. He jest opened them jaws an' snapped 'em once an' it was gone.

"We had been so busy we hadn't noticed, but the crew an' ship's officers had all turned out an' was perched in the shrouds where they could see what was goin' on, an' when the shoat disappeared down that shark's throat, they set up a yell that was sunthin' to hear.

"Well, sir, it must have been a full half-minute that shark jest laid there lookin' pleased with himself, an' I says to myself, says I, 'Good Godfrey, is that critter goin' to digest that there white-hot cannon ball?'

"An' then all at once he give a kind of a lurch, like a big hiccup, an' you could see the shivers travel the whole length of him. He backed away, curled around in a tight half-circle, snapped out straight again, stuck his tail straight up in the air an' went straight down. The bay warn't very deep, so he couldn't go no place in that direction, an' it warn't but a few seconds before he riz again, an' when he come up, he was movin' right along. He went his full length into the air an' come down flat on his guts with a crack that we could feel the whole length of the ship. From then on for three or four minutes no mortal man ever saw the like of the maneuvers that critter went through. It didn't seem possible that flesh an' bone could tie itself into sech knots an' move itself through air an' water in so many different directions at once. The riggin' of the ships in the bay an' the line of the shore was black with people watchin' an' the noise they made, shoutin' an' yellin', was like a fair an' a circus an' an army goin' to war all mixed up in one great sound across the water.

"Finally, after one last great curvin' leap clear of the bay, he made away from us straight for the shore, his back-fin throwin' spray five feet from him on either side. He hit an anchored lighter, riz an' went clean over it an' then tore into shoal water an' skidded high up onto the beach. The crowd scattered when they seen him comin', but when he landed high an' dry, they lit into him with clubs, rocks, spears an' knives an' everything they could lay a hand to. From where we was, they looked like a swarm of ants mountin' onto a big, squirmin', grey worm. They said they was a hole in his belly as big as my arm, where the shot burned through, but I never seen it. I wisht poor old Bowles could have seen it. He went ashore that same day, but it was to go in his grave an' he never saw anything."

I followed my grandmother's lamp through the cold hall, one of my grandfather's nightshirts dragging at my heels, and climbed the steep stairs to the little room under the eaves. It was still colder there and smelled of dust and chamber pots, but the feather bed was deep and soft and I was soon warm. But it was a long time before I dozed, and when I finally slept, I dreamed of an enormous snow-white shark rampaging through packed ranks of helpless geese. I awoke sweating and trembling, afraid to go to sleep again until it began to grow light. I was very sleepy when my grandfather came to get me up and I would have been glad to stay in bed had it not been for the goose hunt.

We crossed the stream by the Lower Bridge and climbed the west slope of the Eastern. On the map this small mountain is called Treat Hill, but I have never heard it called anything but the Eastern. It was hard traveling; every small depression was filled with water and under the trees there were banks of melting snow.

This was before the advent of special clothes for every sporting purpose. One's oldest garments were patched, mended and preserved to serve for outdoor activities, and they were usually thin and of cheap quality to begin with.

We had scarcely crossed Parker's pasture and the stone wall dividing it from Drake's piece, when one of my frayed laces parted and I cast a shoe. Hardly had that damage been repaired with a length of fishline when my right-hand garter broke and left that side all adrift. My long drawers, becoming damp from the drip from the trees and the splash from the puddles, began to stretch and sag until the generous surplus covered by my long cotton stockings settled into a decorative but irritating inch-thick doughnut around the tops of my soggy shoes. We entered thick black growth on the east cant of the mountain and encountered more snow. I tried to step in my grandfather's tracks but slipped and slid, and about every third step one of my rubbers would come off. My feet were very cold and getting colder. The drip from the branches ran down my neck. My other garter tore loose from its upper anchorage, and it required the use of both hands to keep my lower rigging from going entirely adrift. If I had not been kept so busy trying to reef up slack, I would have been in a worse state from the wet and cold, but the constant exercise engendered by the near-loss of various accoutrements and the recovery of the same, coupled with an extremely runny nose that also required frequent attention, kept my blood in circulation and, before we had reached our objective, even caused me to work up a light sweat.

We followed an old wood road down through a thicket of pines, and just before we pitched down over the last abrupt slope to the river, my grandfather stopped and made signs for me to be quiet. We were nearly at the level of the river, and the fog and mist were so thick that we could not see more than a hundred feet in any direction. I stood and listened, my mouth wide open with concentration, and then, above the steady drip from the pines, the sharp, arrogant call of a black duck seemed to come almost from under our feet. It must have been some kind of a signal, for before this sound had entirely ceased the air was filled with a bedlam of quacking, gabbling and honking. The cove and the open water beyond were full of waterfowl.

Two hours later we were still crouched beneath an overhanging hemlock, behind a pile of driftwood. The tide had reached its peak and turned, and I had sat, it seemed, forever, seeing nothing except a thick grey bank of mist and fog from which came the splashings, quackings and all the subdued noises made by hundreds of ducks and geese feeling themselves completely free from danger.

My grandfather had rested the barrels of the Greener Gun over a fork in an old stump and sat immovable behind it, hunched in his old brown overcoat, peering out into the cove. I was half frozen and completely miserable, but had managed to keep at least reasonably quiet. A sudden breeze stirred the hemlock over us, showering more icy water upon my already soaked back.

My grandfather's head came up and he snuffed the air like a hound. Another stronger gust and you could tell that it came from behind us out of a fair quarter. The fog began to lift and move. It was no longer a solid mass but layers of drifting wraiths shot through with streaks of visibility. Looking straight out, I could see tufts of dead grass, an ice cake, stained with mud and dirty water, and now and then a glimpse of open water. There was a pothole out there in the marsh in front of us, a little pond of brackish water a hundred yards across at its widest part. Almost in its exact center was a jumble of ice cakes tossed up on a shallow spot and left by the tides. One piece was standing on its edge and, as the fog lifted, out from behind it swam two great geese. The two biggest, fattest, most desirable geese in all the world! The pool was filled with ducks, too, but I did not see them.

My grandfather had capped the nipples when we had first sat down, and now his right hand stole out and softly pulled both hammers back to full cock. His cheek snuggled down against the stock and, with a thunderous bellow, the Greener Gun let go both barrels. I saw the water boil around the geese, over and under and all around them, just before the cloud of powder smoke, shot through with sparks of burning oakum, rolled out and settled down before us. The air filled with shrieking, clamoring birds rising from the marsh, and above the drifting smoke two geese rocketed noisily aloft and wheeled toward the open river. It seemed impossible, incredible, that those two geese had been the ones my grandfather had shot at, but as the freshening breeze lifted both smoke and mist and rolled it away, the black waters of the pond lay stark and empty before us.

Deserted and empty except for a few small feathers that fled along the dark surface and disappeared before my eyes.

For a moment I sat stunned with the enormity and finality of this disaster, and then I realized that my grandfather had not moved or spoken since the shot. He sat hunched over the gun, still in the position of firing, his cheek still pressed to the stock. My heart gave a violent jump and I felt sick. I leaned forward and looked into his eyes which stared straight out over the gun barrels and saw that they were fairly blazing with some sort of emotion. His brows were drawn together in a terrible frown of pain or anger, and then I saw that the tremendous overcharge in both barrels had blown both hammers back to full cock and that the thumb-piece of the left one was driven deep into his cheek. I opened my mouth to howl, but I was numb with terror and, before I could make a sound, my grandfather gathered himself and tore his face away from the stock. The dark blood welled and streamed down into his beard. I began to sweat and there was a queer fluttering humming in my ears. And then my grandfather spoke. He was not a profane man and seldom blasphemed, but in the course of his wanderings here and there upon the surface of the earth he had accumulated as choice a vocabulary of imprecations as ever scorched the withered grass of a duck marsh.

My sickness forgotten, I sat captivated and spellbound while my grandfather mopped blood with the red bandanna from his neck and invoked eternal damnation upon every infinitesimal part of the Greener Gun from the front sight to the buttplate. He included its manufacturer, the mechanics who built it, the iron that went into its making, and the coal that forged the iron.

His references to the gun were somewhat confusing, for directly after referring to "her" as a deceptive canine female of uncertain virtue, he applied other epithets that could apply only to one of the opposite sex. It was all very edifying, if a trifle perplexing, and I was able to store away many admirable words and phrases in my mind for future use.

It was a long and miserable journey home, for me. There was nothing to anticipate except trouble, for my clothes were in a scandalous condition, and I knew with a dreadful certainty that I was in for a bad time. It proved to be even worse than I feared, but this abortive goose hunt actually proved to be the first small crack that gradually widened into a precarious way to freedom. My grandfather would have no more of the Greener Gun. He borrowed my father's old Iver Johnson Champion, a hitherto despised "britch-loader," and late that summer I shot my first rabbit with it.

CHAPTER III

THE first time I ever saw our river my grandfather took me there. I was very small and the river seemed very large. It was not really a river, anyway, but a stream. Everyone called it The River, although the real river lay over the Eastern Mountain, half a day's journey for such short legs as mine.

When I first saw the river, it ran clear and strong under the timber and stone-cribwork of the Upper Bridge and down between the wrecked and rotting pilings and timbers of the original dam. I have heard it said that my great-grandfather, old "Miller" Averill, built the wooden dam when he built his gristmill, but I do not know this to be a fact and there are none of the older people left to tell me of these things. I am sure about the mill, for although there is no trace of it left, when I was a small boy its great weathered hand-hewn beams were still standing and the mill stones were still in place. We used to use the space under the floor to smoke corn silk and elm root and sometimes Sweet Caporal cigarettes. The great stones lie buried now on the original mill-site under tons of rotting sawdust and debris from the sawmill that came later.

There was a great pool below the old dam on the opposite side of the river from the mill, and here the big boys of the village used to swim. They would stand on a smooth slab of shelving granite, with one hand held decorously in front of them and dive cleanly off into the living water, their white bodies flashing down deep into the clear depths.

When I told my mother about the boys, I learned that swimming naked was very bad and sinful, although it did not seem so to me. When I tried it a few years later, I found it to be very pleasant indeed.

There was a short time when the river ran strong and free. One could fish and swim in a dozen bright riffles and pools from the old brickyard hill down to tidewater below the old dam. The bed was of gravel, yellow sand and great rocks and boulders, and most of the town boys spent the greater part of their time during the summer months either fishing, swimming or exploring upstream as far as Flat Rock Falls. It was a long time before I extended my operations that far, but the stretch of water within sight of the village held unlimited possibilities for amusement. In those days there was a steady run of eels, suckers, white perch, alewives, heavy, brilliantly colored trout and, at rare intervals, a great silvery sea salmon. As soon as the spring smelt run was over and the Mayflowers and dandelions bloomed, the trout would begin to come in, along with a few alewives. And from then on through the short summer there would be white perch, bass, and now and then a trout, until one tired of fishing, or found it necessary to put on shoes. It was generally conceded that taking off one's shoes for the warmer months opened the fishing season, while putting them on again indicated that the best of the fishing had passed.

I don't know when the present stone dam was built, and it doesn't matter. There is no place for exact dates or statistics here; they accomplish little anywhere except to effect compilation of the crimes against nature which are paid for, filed, and apparently forgotten. Our mountains are ravaged by axe and fire until their thin coverings of underbrush, loosened by rains and frost, slip from the soaked rocks and rush toward the valleys, leaving the bare bones of the hills exposed. The timbered swamps are a tangle of tops and brush burned and bleached by the summer sun. The springs that feed the brooks dry up; the brooks in turn are transformed into slimy trickles in summer and into raging torrents during the spring and fall. With no regular source of water to feed them the larger streams fill to their banks for a brief period of freshet in the spring and then subside to a series of stinking pools good for nothing except to breed insects. Brooks that have survived the rape of the timber are found full of every noisome thing that civilization can provide, from human sewage to the bodies of dead animals, and all this is a matter of statistics, compiled, assembled and tabulated at the expense of the public who mutter that some day something must be done about it.

For a long time after the stone dam was built, fish continued to come in with the tide. The steady flow of water over the top of the dam seemed to have a mysterious attraction for them and they concentrated in numbers close up against the dam under the falling water. The spray kept the air cool even on the hottest days and when the fish were running several of us spent most of our time there. On the east wall of the dam, where a trickle of water came through the masonry, one could always find a squirming mass of tiny elvers working their way up the slippery rock toward the pond above, and although at this time none of us knew of the eel's strange breeding, we marveled that there should be so many of these tiny ones coming in from the sea.

When the craving for slaughter overcame us, there was always the humble sucker. They came up from tidewater and stayed in the pools all summer, and by lashing a cod hook onto a broomstick one could hook them out from under the overhanging rocks in astonishing numbers. They were good for nothing except to satisfy the desire to catch and kill something, although sometimes my grandmother would boil up a mess and feed them to the hens. My grandfather said they were good to eat when taken from very cold water just after the ice went out, and once I brought him a mess which I will speak of later.

Smelting time on our river was something to remember and to look forward to from year to year. It began when the ice went out and the frost was coming out of the roads. People burned their banking brush, and the frogs and toads talked shrilly in the evening while they swarmed and mated in the stagnant pools formed by melted ice and snow. I suffered agonies waiting until I should be old enough to join at least half the male populace of the village in that notable and at times remunerative exodus to the river as soon as the spring freshets subsided. I think I must have been ten years old when my parents decided that I might go with my grandfather a night or two in the week when the tide served right. My grandfather was overjoyed to have me along to tend net for him and made a great fuss over the occasion.

Now to go smelt dipping one has to have certain equipment, the most important of which is the net. I have seen dozens of different kinds of nets up and down the coast, but never any that required so much skill to make or afforded their owners so much pride in possession as these smelt-dipping nets. There were a few skilled net-makers in the village, and any male with a yearning for smelts simply had to have a net. I don't know how much they cost in money, but a good net bow was a work of art and preparing the spruce pole with knife and draw-shave was something for no amateur to attempt. First, one had to go into the woods and cut a straight young spruce about two inches, or at most two and a half inches, at the butt and twenty feet in length. This was peeled and dried perfectly straight in a loft, shaved smooth with crooked knife and draw-shave and sandpapered to smoothness until it tapered from two inches at the butt to an inch or an inch and a quarter on the net end. When finished right, it was light and easy to handle and had considerable labor tied up in it. The bow was made of an ash strip, much as a snowshoe frame is made, and the material was very similar to that found in the bow of a good snowshoe. It was usually about two feet long by a foot and a half in width and filled with a half-inch mesh net about two and a half feet in depth. The width and length of the bow as well as the depth of the net might vary according to the taste of the individual, but not very much. The net end of the pole was fitted into a cross-piece about three inches long to spread the open end of the bow properly, and the free ends were allowed to extend down the pole for six or eight inches for lashing. The finished product looked long and ungainly but was surprisingly easy to handle, and one could feel smelts the second they touched the bow or hit the net.

In addition to the net, it was imperative that one have warm clothes, woolen mittens, a pair of rubber boots and a lantern, for this business had to be done after dark when the fish could not see the net.

One could not just go down to the river and start dipping anywhere. The smelts ran close to shore only where the rocks and gravel formed the right kind of riffles for spawning beds, and these most desirable places were usually preempted by the "regulars" who came early, placed their lighted lanterns on a flat rock by the chosen spot and then retired to the store for conversation until it was dark enough to fish.

My grandfather was not one of those who went completely smelt-crazy during the season, so we had to work upstream until we were nearly under the dam before we could find a suitable place to dip. We floundered over the wet rocks, watching for a good eddy and finally decided on a place where the water came fast over an old wooden flume, a part of the old gristmill that still remained. My grandfather did not think it was a very good place and grumbled profanely about it, but after having placed our buckets on a flat rock, and set the lantern behind us where it would not get tipped over, he handed the net to me and told me to try the first dip of the season—just for luck.

The net was heavy, but I managed to swing it out, drop it under the sluice and let the current help me move it slowly over the gravel, downstream. It seemed early for good results, but most of the smelts on that side of the river must have worked up the shore and into that pocket under the old sluice-way. Almost at once fish began to strike against the bow and slide back into the net until their struggles could be plainly felt through the length of the spruce shaft. When I tried to lift the net from the water, the weight was too much for me, and I had to pull it toward me hand over hand. My grandfather quickly seized the bow as it came in, and although I had lost some of my catch, there were smelts enough left in the net to nearly fill one of our buckets.

This was terrific, and I fairly capered with joy. We would have considered ourselves lucky to have been able to get three or four smelts at a dip, and here, in an unknown and untried spot, we had evidently got into a closely packed school that had commercial possibilities.

"Ha," said my grandfather. "Must be a grist of 'em, and we got to do something about it. You stay here and keep quiet while I take this bucket of fish over to the house and bring back something that will hold a few. Keep the net out of the water and, when I get back, we'll make a killing."

He scrambled up over the steep bank with the pail of smelts, and I stood there in the damp darkness fretting and fuming, waiting for him to return. It seemed a long time, but it was probably no more than ten minutes when I heard him hurrying down over the bank with the empty bucket banging against my grandmother's copper wash-boiler.

Ah, that was a great night! We filled both buckets and nearly filled the boiler with icy, silvery smelts before we exhausted the pocket. And long before the time set for me to go home we were done fishing and were trying to get the catch up through the rocks and bushes to the road. I went home and got my express wagon and trundled the load of fish triumphantly to my grandfather's house. We kept the two bucketfuls to eat and give away, but my grandfather sold the contents of the boiler to one of the commercial fishermen for five cents a pound. I had half the money for my own, a whole dollar.

I dipped smelts out of our river many times after that, but only once did I find them in the same place and in such quantities. The river bed has changed now, the old flume is gone and I would not know where to swing my net. Perhaps when the frogs begin their piping in the spring, I may borrow a net and try it again as there is nothing like spring-run smelts from the Penobscot for good eating.

You take them fresh out of water when they are still firm and cold, cut off their heads and, if you are fussy, take out the insides. Then you wash them in cold water, wipe them off with a dry cloth, roll them in corn meal and brown them slowly in an iron skillet with plenty of pork fat. When properly done, you can run a knife down the back, lift out the backbone and have two halves on your plate with no bones to trouble you. After dealing with about a dozen seven- or eight-inch fish, two large baked Maine potatoes well covered with butter, and half a dozen of my wife's hot biscuits, one is apt to feel like resting a little before tackling the dessert, no matter how tempting it may be.

I am quite sure that I will borrow that net and try the smelts again next spring.

In those days the river, with its strong flow of clean water out into the brackish tide of the Penobscot, often had strange visitors. Sometimes while we were fishing or sitting quietly on a great boulder watching the tide come in, we would catch a glimpse of an unknown fish. The smelt nets would often bring in a trout, a struggling slimy eel, or a great flopping sucker, hard and cold, fresh from the salt water. My grandfather ate almost everything that came from the water and, though I brought him many suckers during the summer, he always complained that they were too soft and were only fit to eat very early in the spring. As I became older, I learned that this business of eating suckers was simply a pose with him, something to make conversation, and that he had no intention of cooking and eating any suckers. One spring I caught two very large ones in the dip-net and, since the river was still rimmed with ice in some places, I brought them to him all cleaned and scaled and with the comment that, since the water could not be any colder without freezing, the fish must be in prime condition. He was caught and he knew it, but he managed to appear properly grateful and enthusiastic and invited me to a sucker dinner next day.

My grandfather's house was just across the street from the school building, and when I got out at noon, there was a fishy odor in the air that could be plainly detected as coming from my grandmother's kitchen. One didn't have to sniff to locate it; it could almost be *seen*.

The kitchen was full of pork fat and sucker smoke, and when my grandmother took the fish out of the skillet, they came out in the form of a great pile of bones and meat that looked like some kind of a horrible hash. There was an enormous platter of the mess, and although my grandfather tried to appear eager to get at it, he took more than his usual time to sugar his tea, butter a biscuit and get squared away for action. Finally he hauled the platter over to him, scraped off a plate of the nauseous mess and shoved the platter over to me. I took my own good time about helping myself and watched him closely.

At last, not being able to put it off any longer, he slid his knife blade into the rubble, lifted a good load into his whiskers, chewed hopefully for a moment and then began to erupt sucker bones. He tried to swallow, but couldn't manage it, and suddenly pushed back his chair, walked over to the stove, lifted the cover and spit out the mouthful into the fire. He sat down at the table, rinsed his mouth with a great gulp of tea and then turned on my grandmother:

"Goddammit, Mary," he roared, "you never *could* learn to fry a sucker."

My grandmother said nothing, but she moved quick. She reached the table in one long stride, picked up the platter, opened the door and threw suckers, platter and all, out into the back yard. We ate beans for our dinner.

Both my grandparents were fond of eels and these were often on the table. It was a long time before I could bring myself to eat them, for they were slimy and repulsive when they came from the water; and even after they were skinned and cut in pieces they would squirm and roll about in the frying pan. My grandfather kept at me until at last I tried them and found them very good. So for at least one summer I ate them regularly. I ate them until that day when we found the dead horse out on the mud flats off the South Branch, and since that time I have never been able to stomach them. The horse was partially submerged, so we had to bring our boat up close to investigate. It did not look very good and smelled worse, and when my grandfather poked its swollen belly with an oar, eels came squirming and hustling out of the bloated carcass. They slithered out of the nostrils, the mouth, and every natural orifice and, after one horrified look, I leaned my head over the side of the boat and lost my dinner. I moaned and retched in awful misery, while my grandfather laughed until the tears rolled down his cheeks, because what I was getting rid of so freely was mostly fried eel.

I don't know what strange force or whim of nature guided the lampreys into our river those two years that they came. One year we found a lone eel and during the next two they swarmed in by the hundreds. We caught the first one stranded in a small pool when the tide went out, and no one in the village knew what it was. The village authority on fishes pronounced it a young sturgeon, but as he was known to bear false witness quite freely, we were not satisfied. We were afraid of it—repelled by the sickly yellow of its belly and the yellow teeth imbedded throughout the sucking slit of a mouth. No such thing had ever been seen in the river before, but it was easily identified in the school dictionary when someone finally thought to look for it there. There was a picture of it among the fishes in the back of the book.

We called them "lampers" and slaughtered them joyfully by the hundreds when they came in under the dam. As I remember, they came late in June, and dozens of them, some three feet long, would swim up on a rock ledge at one end of the dam where the water was scarcely deep enough to cover their backs. There they would fasten themselves to the smooth ledge with their sucker mouths and lie with their backs out of water until we tore them from the rock with our hands or battered them with rocks or clubs. We fashioned gaffs by filing the barbs from cod hooks and lashing them to broomsticks, and with these we hooked them from the ledges and flung them struggling and writhing out onto the hot, dry rocks. We slaughtered them by the hundreds that first year, but they came the next spring in even greater numbers. The thing became a town scandal. Rotten carcasses filled the river below the dam, clouds of flies hung over the rocks and ledges, and when the wind was east the stench of death and corruption hung over the main street of the village. The ebbing tides took away some of the filth, but the whole river from the dam to half a mile below it was thoroughly polluted. We fouled our fishing places, spoiled our swimming, glutted ourselves with senseless killing, but still the great eels came and we killed them as long as they stayed.

They were new and strange to us. We feared them

and did our best to exterminate them. It was said that if they once fastened to your flesh they would suck and grind with those horrible yellow teeth until they ate right through you, but we gave them no chance to fasten to anything. Only once did any of us pause to wonder why they came or where they came from and feel a slight twinge of pity for them. Once, lying on a flat rock and looking down into the clear water, I saw two of them working to make some kind of a nest. I do not know if it is a natural habit of these eels to do this, or if the act was something unusual, but I saw them swimming about busily picking up small pebbles in their mouths and placing them on the stream bottom in a small area. If these two were getting ready to spawn, then I still do not understand what all those other eels were doing while fastened to the rock ledge in shallow water. But the sight of the two lampreys building their nest rather spoiled my enjoyment of the slaughter.

The price of pulpwood soared. The farmers sold their wood-lots and timber, crews came and let daylight into the swamp. Blaisdell Brook dried to a trail of rocks through the slash and the remaining hardwood. The great springs deep in the forests became smaller and smaller until they were nothing but caked mud with a few wilting aquatic plants around the margins. The timber came down the stream in the spring, but after a time there was not enough water to run the saw-mill. It stopped going over the dam and what was left became thick and smelled. For days at a time, when the water had been used up at the mill, the pond lay nearly empty, the bottom covered with mud and slime and rotting logs. The ledges and pools below the dam grew warm and stagnant, and a family of mink caught all the fish that were left in the deep hole up under the masonry. After a time the fish stopped coming in with the tide.

Our village was built along the stream and was entirely surrounded by hills. The Eastern Mountain lay just across the river on the east, and on the west a series of foothills rose up from the deep little valley to blend with the slopes of Mount Waldo. All around us were the steep, rocky hills with a gentle slope on one side and rough slides and ledges on the other. It is a tough and rugged country, the hills mostly solid granite with a variable coating of arable soil. In those days the Eastern was thickly covered with pine, spruce and fir with a sprinkling of hemlock. There was some pasture land and one old farm, but now the west slope has been completely cleared into blueberry land, as has the east slope of Mount Waldo.

Those settlers who cleared the land might have wrung enough to eat from the rocky fields but not much else, for later generations found the life too hard. There are hundreds of abandoned fields and orchards, now grown up to alder and grey birch, and others grown over so completely with both hard and soft woods that one can only trace the original fields by the stone walls. The old wells and cellars, stoned up and walled with granite, can still be found, but some of them are almost completely hidden by trees or brush.

Some of these old stone walls are outstanding examples of slow hand labor, and it hardly seems possible that one family could move and pile up so many rocks. My grandfather said these walls were built mostly on rum and that no man in his right senses would ever undertake such a task cold sober. He said that most of these farmers had large families of boys, sometimes six or seven of them, and that on cold wet days the head of the family would invest fifty cents in a couple of gallons of West Indies rum and the grown and half-grown males would all take to drinking rum and piling rocks.

There are any number of roads, once fit for horse travel but now mere traces through the encroaching alders, that will lead to old fields and orchards still open, but good for nothing except for game cover. You can walk for miles on such trails, but wherever you go, if you get anywhere at all, you will have to go either up or down hill. And wherever you travel along the ridges the granite of the hills will break through the thin soil, and you can see the tracks of the Devil's wheelbarrow where its wheel burned its way deep into the solid stone. They say that he was not satisfied with the way Mount Waldo was built and spent considerable time tearing out great slabs of rock and wheeling them to different locations. The slabs of granite are there in proof, also the places where they were torn from the mountain.

There are many deer in the woods and swamps around the village today, but in these early times they were very scarce. Killing one was something to talk about around the stoves at the village stores during the long winter evenings, and very few of them were shot. I think, however, that around 1910 and 1911 there were more grouse in the covers near the village than were ever seen in one locality. I have hunted partridge many years and shot them in many different places, but never again will I see them in such numbers as there were then. Rabbits were the same—and grey squirrels until the Italians at the granite works found that there was free meat for the taking, and they took about all of the squirrels.

Out around the base of Mount Waldo, at Kinney Hook, the grouse ranged in flocks. It was nothing to see six or eight birds go up at once, and around the old orchards and under the lone apple tree in the alder thickets a good shot could have killed a dozen birds in as many minutes. After I became free to hunt, some of us hunted every day we could possibly go, but we shot very few birds. None of us was properly trained, and unless we could catch a bird sitting on the ground or in a tree, they were usually quite safe.

However, it was a long, wearisome time before I was given full freedom to roam the woods and climb the mountains, and I knew the river long before I learned the hills. There is a time in a boy's life when things seem very difficult. He is not old enough to be allowed much freedom, but is beyond the stage where he is satisfied with childish play. I began to read very young and read everything I could get my hands on, and this passed away some of the time.

Those were the days of G. A. Henty, Ralph Henry Barbour, Young Wild West, Fred Fearnot, The Deer Foot Series and *St. Nicholas Magazine*. There were silk flags in Zira cigarettes, and a brand called American Beauties sold for a nickel a pack. Teddy Roosevelt promised to be a great president. There was no question as to the greatness of the U.S.A. Everyone seemed to agree that it was the finest richest nation on earth, and any rash statement to the contrary was likely to result in a poke in the nose. George Washington never told a lie. Benedict Arnold was the world's greatest traitor. The Tories during the Revolutionary war were very nasty people. And all a boy had to do was to go to school and Sunday school reguarly, learn the Ten Commandments and obey them, abide by the Golden Rule, and he could grow up to be President, chief of police or even a big league ball-player.

Sunday was the longest, dullest day in the week. There was church, Sunday school, then a big dinner one had to eat dressed up in tight clothes and a starched collar. Sometimes there would be company and that made things even more complicated. After dinner there was nothing to do, especially in winter, except sit quietly and read some dull book suitable to the holiness of the day, and usually, through some slip in deportment, that book was the Bible. Catholic boys went to church early in the morning and then had the rest of the day to do as they pleased; but according to my mother, it was a sin not to remember the Sabbath Day and to keep it holy all day long. Sometimes on a fine day in the summer we went for a walk, but it was not much fun harnessed up in a Buster Brown collar and tight shoes, so usually one squirmed through the day somehow and put in the week dreading the next one.

Sex was something not even to be thought about. My first insight into the mysteries of birth gave me the impression that there was nothing very complicated about it, and for a long time I firmly believed that if pussywillows were put under a cat they would hatch out into kittens. My grandfather explained the miracle of the pussywillows to me and I tried it out successfully. It happened rather slowly and I had almost given up hope, when one fine morning, sure enough, there were four little squirming lumps of cat in the basket instead of the pussywillows I had put there. I had made a set for five, but my grandfather quickly explained that sometimes they didn't all hatch—like a setting of hen's eggs.

I was delighted with this discovery, but was somewhat hurt and surprised that my mother seemed rather angry at the news. She remarked to my father that it was silly for my grandfather to tell me such absurd things and that I was still more silly to believe them, but my father only laughed and asked her what better method she had to offer for producing kittens and, if she had one, he would like to hear her explain it to me. Of course, later on I learned the difference between fact and fancy, but I never told my grandfather, for I did not wish to disillusion him.

Somewhere between the bow-and-arrow and shotgun period I remember that I began to feel a mild interest in the opposite sex, but it was impossible to form much of an opinion about girls from casual observation, for even when they went "bathing" in the pond, they were swathed in voluminous folds of old woolen dresses that were even more concealing than the frills of their regular attire. One could get a general idea of the female form from the women's department in the Sears Roebuck catalogue, but it was not a good idea to get caught browsing in that section of the book by one's parents.

My mother sneaked up on me one day and, from the resulting lecture, I began to have suspicions that women were a singularly doubtful and dangerous paradox that might lead to all kinds of trouble. This suspicion was very soon to be established as a fact, for upon being elected to represent my Sunday school at the State Y.M.C.A. convention, some of the facts of life were presented to me with a vehemence that was nothing less than devastating.

After the shouting orator had related how great athletes and youths of brilliant intellect had been reduced to physical wrecks with no ambition or stamina just from *thinking* about girls "way down here"—and he would pass his hand rapidly back and forth just below his belt—I began to realize what a hellishly dangerous world I had been born into. And instead of taking the twenty-five cents that had been given me for spending money and squandering it in the glittering brothels of Bangor, I immediately and hurriedly, lest I begin thinking about women, took it to a hardware store and blew the works on ten cents' worth of number two shot and a box of shotgun shell primers.

Strangely enough, after hearing that series of lectures, I began to get curious about those deadly qualities embodied in the female sex, but that was the summer the lampreys came up the river, and my mind became otherwise occupied. War and slaughter seem to be fine substitutes for sex.

I cannot remember when I was not fascinated by the flight of a propelled missile and with my grandfather's aid I spent a great deal of time making bows of different woods, crossbows which we called bow-guns, and inventing and improving arrows and bolts to shoot in them. I sold twenty packages of gold-eye needles and obtained a single-shot air rifle, and learned how much trouble and grief a small boy could experience through the use of one of those inventions of the Devil. It is a thing of springs and tubes that has no accuracy and shoots with just enough force to break a window or raise a blood-blister on human flesh. Mine proved a source of tears and trouble, incapable of instilling even the rudiments of correct training, and an incentive to carelessness because of its inadequacies. I had one of the one-thousand-shot varieties later on and did only about one third as much damage as I was capable of doing because I was in possession of the thing only about one third of the time. There was a locked closet in our house that I never was able to enter.

As fast as one warlike implement was taken from me, I made another. Most of my companions were satisfied with a green hemlock limb for a bow and cedar or pine shafts for arrows, but my bows had to be of seasoned ash, worked down to where I could bend and string them. I made arrows out of white maple and birch, scraping them down with pieces of glass and sandpapering them until they were silky smooth. They were fletched so they would spin in flight and, although I knew nothing at all of conventional archery, I practiced until I could shoot quite accurately. I designed a bolt for one of my bow-guns that would spin, too, and inserted a filed clapboard nail in its head so that the iron protruded about an inch. This proved to be a very accurate and hard-shooting weapon, and I distinguished myself with it by nailing my younger brother's upper lip to his gum at a distance of almost a hundred yards. A very satisfactory performance as a demonstration of range and accuracy, but quite painful to both of us. I think I suffered more than my brother, because I had to watch that new bow-gun and all the bolts for it broken up and burned in the kitchen stove, while my brother grinned evilly at me when my mother's back was turned and howled dismally whenever she glanced in his direction.

Just before I began taking my father's old shotgun from my grandfather's house and really going hunting, the situation at home had become almost unbearable. It seemed that the only thing one was allowed to do without being scolded was to go to school, Sunday school and church. My mother was not well; she worked and worked and fretted and scolded all day and far into the night. Hanging around the corner with the other boys was forbidden. Loafing in the barber shop or around the front of the pool room was nothing less than criminal. If I stayed home and read, my mother complained that I was bone lazy and always had my nose stuck in a book. If I got loose and indulged in a little rock throwing or snapping green apples from the sharpened end of a limber switch, I was sure to wing somebody or break a window. My clothes were always getting torn, I wore out expensive shoe leather, and, in short, I was nothing but a somewhat skinny liability to the family. I was unlucky and miserable. I ached for freedom, but did not know how to use it when I had it; so I spent hour upon hour, day upon day locked into my room with bread and water for my meals and the Bible for amusement. I became sulky and rebellious,

took up the use of tobacco with astonishing ease and learned to inhale from a strong pipe in no time at all. At the end of a period of questionable freedom I would come home reeking with the fumes of Central Union cut plug which the chewing of cedar failed to conceal or even dull, and then the storm would break anew. I would be sent up to my room for two or three more days of deadly dreariness, confined to the door-yard for a week or more, and there were long days, even weeks, when my parents refused to speak to me at all.

I think that at this time I was not quite twelve years old—and I was a criminal. My mother wept and called upon God to witness the acts of the viper that she had nourished in her bosom and begged that when I got my just deserts I might be spared the noose and merely sent to State Prison. Hardly a day went by that I was not threatened with reform school and sometimes my clothes were all packed for my departure. During this time of tribulation I must have spent the better part of the summer vacation in confinement and disgrace, and my spirits sank so low in realization of my worthlessness that I could look nobody in the eye. Sometimes I caught my father looking at me with something in his eyes that might have been compassion, but, being of the same blood and disposition, we both kept bitterly silent.

The next year things were better. There were quantities of wild blueberries on the Eastern and I was allowed and even encouraged to go berrying. When they ripened the last of July and the first weeks in August, I would take my five-quart pail, pick up the shotgun at my grandfather's house and go up on the mountain for the day. Sometimes I became interested in exploration and in chasing the crows and failed to fill my pail, which was bad. Other days I filled my pail quickly and then roamed over the mountain for the rest of the day, which was good.

The shotgun was too long and heavy for me, the stock had a tremendous drop and, with the old blue Winchester New Rival shells or those of my own loading, it made an ungodly noise and kicked my thin, boney shoulder painfully. It had a short low hammer that was hard to cock. To break the gun open one pressed down on the trigger guard which was bent up and flattened for a thumb-piece; and it was so old and loose that it sometimes flew apart when it went off. I thought it the best gun in the world, and since it shot a good even pattern of coarse shot like BBs or number twos, I could do all right with it by resting it on a fence rail or a limb. I learned not to chase crows and let them come to me, and one memorable day, as I hid under a big pine, a scout came over to locate me and got a charge of BBs that folded him up in the air and dropped him almost at my feet. That was a day to remember. I had shot a bird—flying!

Rabbits were easy. The mountain was covered with them, and one had only to creep through the pines and spruces or work through the small softwood growth in the pastures to send them scurrying, or better still to shoot them sitting. I brought quite a few to my grandfather, who praised me highly and converted them into his famous rabbit stew.

This pride in me and in the rabbit stew came near being the cause of my downfall, but, as it happened, turned out to be my salvation. One evening in September my grandfather came to our house with a pail of stew for my mother. I remember quite clearly that it was on a Monday evening; my father was just washing up for supper and my mother was setting the table.

She took the stew and said, "Why, papa, where did you get the rabbit? I thought you were laid up all last week with a touch of rheumatism in your bad leg."

"Hell," said my grandfather jovially, "I don't have to hunt no more. The boy gets all the rabbits I need, and some to give away."

I guess maybe he had been to the cellar-way just before he came. Anyway the minute the words were out, his jaw dropped and his face was a study in consternation. My own face flamed and cold sweat broke out all over me.

My mother's face set in grim lines as she took the pail of stew and went into the pantry with it. My grandfather looked at me appealingly, but I knew I was lost and that the situation was hopeless. All through September I had done so well at school and behaved so well at home that my Saturday roamings had gone unquestioned, and now owing to a slip of the tongue—well, anything could happen.

My mother returned from the pantry and resumed the business of setting the table, but in a deep silence that could mean only one thing—she was leaving it to my father to deal with me. My father finished scrubbing the stone dust from his face and strode into the kitchen from the pantry. He looked hard at me and I began to shake.

"Did you tell your grandfather that I said it was all right for you to take the gun?"

I said, "No, I didn't tell him anything. I just went and took it. I knew he didn't care."

My father looked at my grandfather and said, "That right, George?" And my grandfather said, "Yes, and I be damned if I see any harm in it. While he's in the woods, he's off the streets." And my father said, "Well, I'm inclined to agree with you, but you know how it is, George, and thanks for the stew."

Well, my grandfather knew what that meant so he wished us a polite good evening and went sorrowfully home.

After he had gone, my mother came out of the pantry, went upstairs to her room and began to cry. My father sat down in his own special chair in the corner and made a cigarette. It was awful. Here was supper all ready to be eaten, the table all set, and my mother upstairs having a spell. I stood there in the middle of the kitchen floor and wished I could die and go straight to hell and be done with it.

My father put a match to the cigarette, inhaled, and blew out a cloud of smoke toward me.

"What in God's name," he said pleasantly, "am I going to do with you?"

I fought down a rising panic and said desperately, "I can't see where I have done anything very bad." And then added hastily, "I didn't mean to talk back."

He dragged deeply on the cigarette. "Well, I asked you a question and expected some kind of an answer. I'm going to take a chance, a long one. You like that old gun?"

I stated fervently and with much emphasis that it was

without doubt the best shooting gun in the whole town and perhaps the State of Maine.

He said, "Well, it used to be quite a weapon, but it's seen its best days. After supper you better go get it and bring it home, so we'll know where it is and when it goes out and comes back. You go get it and bring it here and then I'm going to take it down to the shop and tighten it up. And then—well, I'm going to give it to you. I'm going to let you have it for your own and with it a dozen brass shells that I have hidden away. The shells will be yours too, and a pound of powder, some primers, a wad-cutter and some loading tools, so you can load your own shells. I am going to give you the gun and these other things, but you have got to begin now to keep out of trouble. If you are old enough to shoot meat for the pot, you are old enough to have a gun, *but* you'll have to learn to use a little judgment and learn, too, that when you get the things you really want, you most always have to give up something in return. The gun will be yours and yours alone, and you will be given plenty of time to hunt with it, but in return for these privileges, you must learn that you can't run the ridges *all* the time and you will have your chores to do around the house. I never could understand why you will work all day for your grandfather and seem to enjoy it, when you can't seem to fill the wood box two or three times a day at home. You know what needs to be done around here and from now on you go ahead and do it without having to be told. You do this and behave yourself and we'll get along all right."

He paused reflectively and put down the dead cigarette. "There may be times when you feel that you have to go hunting, but if you stop and think it over, it might come to you that you could save trouble by putting it off for another day. You can't always have things as you would like them, and your mother is not well. She gets upset over nothing and we have to humor her."

This was a long speech for my father to make, for he was known to be very close-mouthed. The words sank deep into my mind and filled me with joy and a determination to do as he wished. I continued to get into difficulties now and then, but from that day on I was never judged until my side of the story was heard and I was seldom punished unjustly.

That night my father and I ate our supper alone, and late into the night I could hear the voices from the bedroom where my mother pleaded and argued angrily long after we should all have been asleep. I could not hear all of the talk, but I did hear enough to know that she was bitterly opposed to my having the gun and at the last I heard my father say wearily but firmly: "You'll never learn that a man has to have a chance to get around by himself and be alone once in a while. You've nagged him and I've beat him and none of it has done any good. If he stays home and reads, you say he does nothing but stick his nose in a book. If he plays ball with the boys, he is running with a gang of hoodlums. If he sits quietly—and God knows what he is thinking when he does that—you say he is sulking. You complain because he likes his grandfather better than he does us, but what in God's name have we ever done to make him like us?"

My mother cried out that she would not be sworn

at and went into the spare room, and after that it was quiet.

My father was mistaken about my not liking him, for I loved him dearly; and in later years when he went away, not to return to our village until I brought him home to die, and people wondered about it, I remembered what he said about a man having to be alone once in a while.

After I became a man and my mother married again, she held me up as a shining example to all men. My mother often said that during my youth I never once caused her a moment's grief or trouble.

CHAPTER IV

THERE were some picturesque characters among the old men of the village. Many of them had gone to sea for a living, fishing off the Grand Banks or sailing across the great oceans to foreign lands. Thin and bent and crippled with rheumatism, they would hobble from their little homes to sit a while in the sun or huddle around the hot stoves in the village stores, smoking their strong pipes and spinning yarns that grew a little with each telling.

There was Old John Norton, who pulled my first loose tooth. Mr. Norton was one of the last of those fabulous hunters who roamed over New England hunting, fishing and selling small necessities to farm women along the way. He carried these in a pack on his back and some people mistakenly thought him nothing but an old peddler. He was a gifted teller of strong tales, and in later years many of his original yarns have been credited to others and appeared in print.

The first time I ever saw him he pulled that tooth, and I never forgot the experience. My mother had bought some small article from him and, like a good salesman, he had to please her by remarking what a fine lad I seemed to be. My mother said that no doubt I was no worse than average but at the present moment

I was being bad. She explained that I had fallen and loosened one of my front teeth and would not let her pull it out. Whereupon Mr. Norton proceeded to hypnotize me. That is the only way I can describe the proceedings because, through some mysterious force that he exerted upon me, I suddenly found myself sitting on his knee and shortly thereafter there was a piece of stout linen thread attached to the tooth. At this point, I revived a bit and began to rebel, but he assured me that he had no intention of yanking that string until I got good and ready to let him. Meanwhile he would tell me a story about a huge trout that he had caught last week out in the Meadow Brook. He had a very soft and convincing way of speaking, and I sat there on his knee with my mouth hanging open and the piece of thread dangling out of it while he went on with his story:

"This here trout," he began, "was an old one an' I'd been tryin' years and years to ketch him. Two or three times I hooked onto him, but he always got away. So this day I crept up to the edge of the hole an' looked down under the tree roots an' there he was, a-layin' there on the gravel a-fannin' the water with his fins an', boy, he was handsome sight! So I watched him a while an' then dropped a fat worm down in front of him. That worm was pink an' fat an' plump an', in fact, one of the prettiest worms I ever saw, but that old trout never paid any mind to it. Then I tossed in a big grasshopper, but he didn't have no appetite for that either an' I says to myself, says I, 'John Norton, this here trout has got to come out of there an' there is jest one way you can do it.' So I slid back from the edge of the pool an' got me a short piece of stout alder about two foot long an' onto it I tied a piece of copper wire about four foot long an' in the end of the copper wire I made me a runnin' noose with an openin' into it jest a little bigger than the trout's belly. Then I wiggled up to the edge of the pool again, reached out easy-like an' dropped the noose down in front of his nose. He kind of backed away from it, but then he stopped an' I jest eased it over his head until it lay jest back of the gills. An' then I got both hands onto the stick, braced myself and give the most ungodly yank you ever see an' out came the trout floppin' onto the grass."

Foolishly absorbed in the story, I had not noticed that Mr. Norton had gained possession of the end of the string hanging out of my mouth, and when he came to the place where he "gave that most ungodly yank," he did just that, and there I sat minus the tooth and watching it dangle at the end of the thread. I thought that I had been vilely tricked and made a fool of, but when I told my grandfather about it, he laughed until the tears ran down his cheeks.

There was considerable rivalry among these patriarchs, and it was amusing to see how one would maneuver to get the best of an argument. Although our town was strictly prohibition as was the rest of the State, we had a tavern that sold liquor. There was no secret about this, and in consequence many of the oldtime drummers liked to land up in town over the week end instead of going home. There was a fine livery stable connected with the tavern, so, with refreshment and transportation at hand in case of emergency, one could relax in comfort. The Upper Bridge crossed the stream a stone's throw from the hotel and on sunny afternoons one could usually find two or three of the traveling men loafing on the bridge in company with several of the local gentry who tagged along in case there should be "sunthin' on the hip." These would vie with each other in the telling of tall tales and bits of amusing local gossip, and in due time would be rewarded with "jest a small swaller" to lubricate the vocal cords and keep them tuned to the right conversational pitch.

One Sunday afternoon John Norton, Charles Milliken and several drummers were enjoying the sun, when John looked over on West Hill, about a mile and a half from the bridge, and called attention to a great boulder that perched on the top of the ridge.

"There, gentlemen," he began, "jest twenty year ago I stood right here in this same spot an' shot probably the biggest buck ever killed in the State of Maine. Stood right here in this identical spot an' shot him right through the head. He was standin' on that big rock you see, gentlemen, over there on top of the hill."

This was too much for Mr. Milliken and he lit into John, hammer and tongs: "If you *must* lie, John, why don't ye tell sunthin' reasonable? Ye know danged well, even if ye could see the deer over the sights at that distance, the bar'l never was bored that would throw lead that fur."

Mr. Norton was somewhat taken aback, but only for an instant. He sidled over toward Mr. Milliken and laid a remonstrative hand upon his arm. "Now I did so, Charlie. I shot that deer jest like I told it, an' I'll tell you what gun I did it with. I shot that buck with that old long-bar'l muzzle-loadin' Lancaster rifle that belonged to your father."

Ridge Runner

Mr. Milliken straightened his rheumatic old back and fairly beamed: "Well, why in hell didn't ye say so in the fust place? Ye might have done it with *that* gun all right."

Some of the younger men were fairly good, too, but I cannot recall which one of them it was who explained so ably why he loaded the shells for his old 1894 model Winchester 38-55 with different charges of powder. He was at his loading bench charging and carefully segregating the finished cartridges into different lots. Somebody asked him what the idea was, and he explained that it was a simple matter of velocities. He did not give out any ballistical data, but informed his questioner that his technique demanded one fast load and one a little slower. He said that he was fairly proficient in the operation of a lever action Winchester and ordinarily figured on keeping his bullets about two feet apart in the air. Fast shooting, together with the method of loading, produced something quite unique in the line of moving projectiles:

"It's this way. I load a fast one and then a slow one into the magazine and that leaves me with a slow one in the chamber to start out with. Well, sir, I was down to Washington County huntin' a couple of years ago an' in the middle of one of them big burns up gets an old rauncher of a buck about three hundred yards off. He run right broadside to me, so I led him a foot or so an' begun to throw lead jest as he come opposite a big dried-out stump. He come up to that there stump an' then stopped, kind of leanin' up against it with his head droopin' down an', thinks I, that's a pretty sick deer, so I don't waste no more lead on him. I shoved some more shells into my rifle an' started walkin' toward him, but he never moved a hair—jest stayed right there leanin' up against that stub. Warn't nothin' else he could do because he was deader than a hammer an' nailed right to that dry hardwood with a good eight inches of solid lead. Them bullets had nosed into each other somewhere along the line."

The fall after my father gave me the gun, I hunted the flocks of partridges that ranged from the lower slopes of Mount Waldo to the edge of the big swamp north of the West Hill. There was just time after school to walk up the railroad track a mile or so, cut up across the east slope of the hill through the alder runs and thorn bushes and come home by the dirt road that runs from the top of the hill down into the village.

This was the week day hunt, but Saturday afternoons I went out around the foot of the mountain. There were birds by the hundreds and I shot what shells I could afford with little result. Even when I knew there were grouse under a thorn bush or under an apple tree and got all braced for the shot, the thunder of wings would bring the gun halfway to my shoulder and away would go the charge into the ground or somewhere wide of the mark. Nowadays a boy would receive a little training on moving objects before being turned loose in the field, but I had to learn by the old trial and error method on wild game. There was nobody to teach me wing shooting because there were very few good wing shots in our locality. One of the more successful hunters had a small dog which would flush grouse into trees where they would perch foolishly and watch the dog until the hunter came up and took his shot. Most of the hunters had good eyesight and killed their birds sitting under the apple trees or in the branches.

Probably none of us will ever see the like of the shooting that we had for a few years, but in proportion to the number of shots fired the number of birds brought to bag was very small. The trip after school was necessarily short; the fast walk up the track, the tramp through those marvelous covers and then the road home with cold fingers clamped around the gun and a vast yearning in the stomach. More often than not I reached home empty-handed, but there were impressions left on the mind never to be forgotten. The picture of short strong wings against the autumn sky, a rocketing grouse in wild twisting flight down a lane of crimson and gold, and often the heart-stopping confusion of several birds flushing at once offering so many chances that no shot at all was fired.

At the last of the season, when the birds went up strong and high against the pattern of the leafless trees, I had another picture to remember. I shot my first game bird flying, as clean and perfect a shot as ever was made. One of the young men of the village, who would have become an expert hunter had he lived, took the trouble to listen to the sum of my woes and tell me what was wrong with my shooting. He explained the importance of bringing the gun fully to the shoulder, so that the sighting plane would be automatically over the barrel, and the necessity of holding close on to the bird even though the shotgun did scatter its load. He told me something of shot patterns and how the charges of smaller shot often killed cleaner than the larger pellets because of the denser patterns, and I bought two loads of number fours to try out the theory.

A few evenings later I put up a bird in the open and on the rim of a pasture. It flushed close, and at the whirr of wings I poked the gun out ahead of me as usual, but checked myself in the nick of time. It seemed ages before the stock touched my cheek and I could swing the muzzle to cover the bird, but at the heavy report of the black powder it crumpled in the air and fell almost straight. I have shot many birds since then, but not even the infrequent thrill of a double can equal seeing that bird fall from the cold evening air of nearly forty years ago.

Many of the village boys had guns of their own, some of them good but most of them little better than wrecks. By judicious trading an apparently useless weapon could sometimes be made serviceable and fixed up to shoot fairly accurately. I acquired a Stevens .22 with no sights and a bullet stuck in the barrel, and with my father's aid I managed to make an adequate set of sights and remove the bullet from the rifling. While working on this rifle and a single-shot Remington 38 R.F., I learned about the moving of sights to change the bullet's point of impact on the test target; and it was not long before I was busy adjusting sights for half the rifles in town. I traded and worked and loaded shells and read all I could find on the subject of firearms, which was not much. I learned that the surest and best way to get authentic information was to go direct to the large manufacturers of arms and ammunition, and I acquired quite a library of catalogues. I had found a hobby that really absorbed me, and I loved everything connected with it. The smell of gun oil, the waxy smell of new shells just out of the case, the reek of black powder and later the sickish, sweetish odor of smokeless, were all a delightful perfume in my nostrils.

I had to watch my step and be temperate in my hunting, for my mother was not fully reconciled to this state of affairs and sometimes made a fuss over my goings and comings. Once she caught up five new black powder shells that my grandfather had just bought for me and, before I could stop her, had dumped them in the blazing fire box of the kitchen stove. The resulting explosion lifted all the stove lids and filled the immaculate kitchen with soot and ashes. My father was very grim about that, but ruled that it had happened through no fault of mine. All the same, there was a very strained atmosphere around me for quite a few days. Strangely enough, after a short time my mother chose to take it as a joke upon herself and in later years would laugh about it.

I found that the best way to avoid trouble was to do most of my traveling in the woods alone, or be very careful in my choice of running mates. I had one or two companions who could be trusted to behave themselves and thus help to put a brake on my own impulses to mischief, and we usually hunted in pairs.

The situation was a very good example of American youth turned loose with dangerous weapons and very little training in their use. Some one of the crew was invariably nursing a bullet wound, but they were mostly hand and foot injuries and healed up quickly. I collected a .38 long Colt bullet over the heart quite early in my career, and one of my companions took a bullet of the same calibre on the thin bone that comprises the outer side of the right eye socket. Luckily the bullet chose to slide along the bone on the outside and punch a hole in the ear, instead of taking the inner route; and other than causing the boy to be kind of gun-shy for a week or two, it did no real damage. I spent a lot of time afield with this boy with the hole in his ear. He liked the woods almost as well as I did, and we spent many happy days scouting the shore of the Penobscot around the Eastern Mountain, shooting at the herons, shitepokes, and the great hawks that wheeled over the marshes. During the blueberry season we indulged in a game of my invention that nearly caused the end of our beautiful friendship.

After we had filled our pails, we would take our shotguns and two blank shells of my loading, and each would head for a certain predetermined spot on the mountain. When we arrived at our starting point we each fired a shot to show that we were ready and then began to work toward each other through the brush and timber, utilizing all possible cover in a pretty fair imitation of frontier warfare. The one that first got a good look at his opponent and a shot at fair shotgun range was judged to be the winner.

I usually loaded my shells with a standard cardboard and felt base wad, but during a temporary shortage I had cut several experimental wads from one of my grandfather's heavy felt larrigans. One day the shell in my gun was loaded with this innovation ahead of three and a half drams of black powder. Never having had occasion to use this combination before, I had no idea of the wad's combustible or ballistical characteristics.

Ridge Runner

During the course of nearly an hour's slow stalking, it became evident that my cautious friend had established himself on an old game trail winding around the steeper side of the mountain through down timber, boulders and slabs of granite, and was playing a waiting game. So with excellent reasoning and expert woodsmanship I proceeded to get above him and scout along the crest where I could look down on him. My survey of the situation proved to be right, for in a short time I was lying on my stomach watching him as he crouched behind a fallen spruce with his eyes fixed on the trail in the direction from which I was expected to come. I lost no time in training the old Ivor Johnson on his person, but was appalled at the results of the shot. The felt wad sailed out of the muzzle blast trailing a thin stream of smoke, covered the forty yards to the target and dropped none too gently in the somewhat luxurious growth of hair at the back of my unsuspecting victim's neck. Burning hair fused with burning hair, as, with a wild howl of fright and dismay, the recipient of this crude but original incendiary projectile hurdled the blow-down and took off down the side of the mountain. He didn't get burned much, for at about the second wild swipe, he got rid of the blazing wad, but I had a hard time convincing him that the whole business was an accident.

During the first two years that I was allowed to have a gun, deer hunting was forbidden. My father said I was too young to go after such large animals and, to tell the truth, the local hunters were prone to become excited at the sight of a deer and get careless with their rifles. I don't recall that there were any serious accidents, but there were a lot of near misses and at times, when a driven deer broke out into the open between two parties of hunters, the resulting commotion assumed the aspects of a small battle.

My grandfather traded around and got a 38-55 Winchester model '94 rifle in fair condition and went hunting with it two or three times a year, but he was not very keen about killing a deer and muffed the only chance I ever knew him to have. He followed a doe and a lamb down from Dutch Mountain to the edge of the Big Meadow which had flooded and then frozen over, and when my grandfather jumped them at the end of the timber and put them out into the open, they found it treacherous going. He said it was the funniest sight he ever saw, the little deer trying to keep up with the big one, and both of them slipping and sliding in all directions. He sat down on a stump and laughed until he was helpless.

I asked him somewhat indignantly why he didn't shoot one of them and he gave me a blank look. "Well now," he said, "don't that beat hell. I never thought of it."

I got through high school by the skin of my teeth. I hunted, fished, played baseball on the town team, sold the usual magazines, cut and peeled popple, picked up potatoes, hired out to farmers during vacations, and earned enough to buy my clothes and help pay my board. I never did find out what algebra and geometry were all about, but I had the endurance of a hound dog and an appetite that I was ashamed of. I ate and ate, both at home and at my grandfather's, but I was always hungry and, instead of putting on weight, I remained as thin as a skinned owl. My father said carrying so much grub around inside of me wore me down and kept me thin, but the fact was I simply burned it up. If I wanted to go anywhere in a hurry, I ran, and I was in a hurry most of the time. So far as I knew, the only organs inside me were those engaged in the assimilation of food, for heart and lungs functioned so perfectly that they gave no indication of their presence. My body was doing all right, but my brains seemed incapable of acquiring any useful knowledge, or rather the contents of the textbooks that my teachers attempted to cram into it.

My mother was ambitious for me and wanted me to be able to hold down a genteel position such as an office clerk. Such people, in those days, were due a certain amount of deference and lived on a different plane than ordinary stonecutters and quarrymen. The bookkeeper at the granite works received the enormous salary of twenty-five dollars a week, straight time, lived in a big white house and had a driving horse. He wore a dark suit and a white collar every day in the week, and his wife was very gracious, if a mite standoffish. His daughter was very beautiful and fashionable, and his youngest son, although handicapped by his position and the fact that he was smart in school, was interesting company. He could dig things out of the Bible that were quite fascinating and puzzling—things in the Old Testament that I had passed over as being very dull reading. He was quite a lad and in some circles was flatly pronounced to be a hellion. There was a time when I was very close to him—too close, for he was the one who took a snap shot at me with a supposedly empty revolver and caused me no end of trouble while I was recovering from a smashed rib.

But even with this family held constantly before me as an example of success through brains instead of brawn, I could not think of anything more deadly than to be humped over a desk in a stuffy office all day, and during the last two years of school I made up my mind as to what course I was going to take.

CHAPTER V

As a small boy, the map of Maine fascinated me, and it still does. The names of its northern lakes, ponds and rivers roll pleasantly from the tongue and have a musical sound to the ear. Where else can you find a Desolation Brook, a Munsungan Pond, or a Mooseleuk Lake? Some of our men went North on infrequent hunting trips and their reports concerning the country and the game were exciting if somewhat fabulous. Miles and miles of clear waterways through the great forests where a man could travel for days enjoying peace and solitude, hunting and fishing, or just loafing if he cared to do nothing else.

During my last two years in school our principal was discovered to be a surveyor and timber cruiser who worked at this entrancing occupation during the summer, and as he was a man of no small narrative ability, I listened eagerly to his vivid accounts of his wanderings through the tall timber. If I had listened half as attentively to his abortive attempts 'to instil some small knowledge of algebra and plane geometry in my head, I might have "amounted to something," but, being what I was, facts and figures, except as they might be applied to elementary ballistics, merely bounced off my thick skull or slid around it.

One of my former hunting companions, a youth a few years older than myself, got a job as timekeeper for the Great Northern Paper Company, and when his letters began coming in from the Dead River country describing the hunting and fishing in that region, they did a lot toward strengthening my purpose and increasing my impatience.

My grandfather was rather put out with me when I tried to explain my feverish desire to leave home and go North into the big woods.

He said, "What you want to do that for? Hell, you won't see nothin' but a lot o' trees, rumhounds, an' trouble. God sakes, all you've done is run the ridges since you was big enough to trot, an' now you want to make a business of it!"

My statement that I had never seen any *real* ridges or any *real* timber and my attempt to interest him in some of the larger lakes and rivers met with a loud snort.

"Hell, one spruce tree is jest like another. Might be a little bigger or a little smaller, an' these fresh-water puddles you talk about—Bah! If you want water, get a good sound hull under your feet an' two or three damned good oceans ahead of you, ship under a skipper that can whoop an' drive 'er an' sail around the world two or three times an' back again. You got a war to fight pretty soon an' you ain't goin' to get in no condition for it, froggin' around in the brush. Place to fight a war is offen a ship's deck."

I conceded the war to him, but resolved that if I was to do any fighting there would be solid ground under my feet. And besides I wanted to be a ridge runner.

Ridge Runner

When I finally got out of high school in June, 1915, my application for a timekeeper's job had been filed with the Great Northern for nearly six months. It had been filed, and forgotten as I thought, because at that time it seemed that half the young men in the New England States were all bent on working for that company and every last one of them wanted to begin in a clerical capacity.

I could get no assurance or encouragement, so late in August when the men off the summer drives were arriving in Bangor for a delayed fling at the fleshpots, I shipped out as a cookee for the Katahdin Pulp and Paper Company. Teamed up with another boy from home, I went up to Patten, out through the Shin Pond country, across the Seboois River to Lower Grand Lake and across that body of water by motor boat. From the west shore, by putting one foot ahead of the other for many wearisome miles, we progressed to a pulp outfit on the north side of Pogy Mountain due north from Sourdnahunk Lake. It was a mean outfit—board and tarred paper camps—and right at the beginning we struck a bad snag. The office refused to consider our signed contracts as cookees and told us plainly that we could saw pulp or get to hell back down the tote road. Since the only transportation across the lake was by company boat, they thought they had us boxed in, and I have no doubt that they planned it just that way.

We stalled around long enough to get supper, but when it came to a bunk for the night, they wouldn't let my partner and me double up. The hot, stinking camp was bad enough, but when I saw the greasy, bearded foreigner that I was supposed to turn in with and sensed a peculiar gleam in his eye, we both slipped outside and spent an uneasy night in a near-by sawdust pile. We were off before daylight the next morning. They called it a little over ninety miles to Patten and we made it in three days. A leaky canoe and a crude paddle that we "found" a mile or so south of the boat landing enabled us to make a risky crossing of the lake in some of the roughest water that I have ever encountered, but we finally made it with my partner stretched out in the bottom of the canoe in six inches or so of lake water. He was *not* a canoeman but made fair ballast. We had no money, having blown it all in at Bangor before we shipped out, so of course the swing camps that fed us coming in refused to give us any food while we were bound out. We walked, drank spring water when we could find it, tightened our belts and cursed the K.P. outfit until we hit Shin Pond where my partner swapped a gold Waltham watch for a small can of corned beef and a box of crackers. We tore into that grub like starving wolves, filled up the empty spaces with pond water and then lost the whole of it. A very discouraging performance. In Patten we found a man who wanted a couple of hands to pick up potatoes, so we picked what we were able to, rested up for a few days and then a telegram with train fare came from home. My job with the Great Northern was waiting as soon as I could report to Bangor.

    I went home, cleaned up, and made a fresh start. About the time Jamie McGaskil had his famous case in court, I was headed up across Moosehead to Pittston Farm.

The last of the great pine suitable and accessible for masts and spars had been cut. Many of the legendary heroes of the axe and cantdog had moved west following the big timber, but there were still giants, even in my day. The Gilberts, Al McNeil, Tom and Steve Ranney, Bill Curran of the short wood operations and a host of lesser satellites were busily engaged in letting daylight into the swamps and harvesting great stands of spruce for the Great Northern. Jim Sargent built roads reaching out through the North country; telephone lines followed the roads. The company was prosperous, there were jobs of all kinds, and although the supply of skilled woodsmen was diminishing, the scum from the cities had not yet begun to be shipped in.

Over in the Sourdnahunk country Bill Curran was cutting and driving spruce in four-foot lengths and proving that practically unskilled labor, blessed with a strong back and a weak mind, could cut and land pulpwood at the mills more cheaply than skilled woodsmen could cut logs and drive them down the turbulent streams and rivers. The last great long lumber drives were booming through the wooden dams at Canada Falls, Seboomook and Chesuncook, filling the West Branch of the Penobscot with millions of board feet of tossing, grinding spruce. Logging was still an art, but it was soon to become a matter of bent backs, bucksaws and cord measure.

It was a hard life. Men lived and worked like beasts. The food was adequate, according to the times, and plentiful. The welfare of a crew depended mostly on the ability of the camp cook and his helpers, and often ambitious short-order men were shipped in who were totally unfamiliar with the limitations of wood fires and the rigid customs and conventions necessary to the successful conduct of a cook-room. Good material was wasted and sometimes whole crews left such camps in disgust. Men working for a wage of from ninety cents to a dollar and five cents a day should have had the best food available and they knew it.

The bull-cook's "Roll Out" came long before daylight in the cold winter mornings. The long, booming, dismal wail lifted men stiffly from their bough-lined kennels to douse their sleep-numbed heads in icy water. At breakfast call they filed silently into the lamp-lit cook-room, took their accustomed places at the long board tables, turned over their inverted tin plates and cups and proceeded to stoke up with enormous quantities of beans, bread, hot tea and perhaps doughnuts. There was no coffee—that did not come until years later. There was no conversation, no sound except the champing of busy jaws, the subdued rattle of tin and the inhalation of tea. Now and then the cook might speak sharply to a slow cookee, but it was a recognized fact that, in a well-conducted cook-room, talk was strictly taboo. It was a place for the rapid and thorough filling of the stomach and nothing was allowed to happen that would slow the tempo.

Men worked regardless of the cold. A blizzard might hold a crew in camp for a day or two, but no matter how low the mercury dropped the teams went jingling out into the dark before dawn and the men followed. All night long in the dead of winter one could hear the trees cracking like rifle shots. Even the green logs of the camp walls would snap, groan and move in their bedding until the cracks spread and the chinking fell out, letting the bitter cold creep in.

Snowshoes became a necessity and then a curse, for one could not move three feet off the beaten trails without them. Ears and noses froze and peeled. Fingers and hands cracked and refused to heal. Washing and shaving became an effort and sometimes an impossibility, and twice during my first winter I rolled and tossed upon my bunk for days at a time, tormented with the tortures of snow-blindness.

Steel became brittle and broke, the frosty wood of the standing trees became filled with ice and often played vile tricks upon the cutting crews. Men were sometimes killed or maimed through the agency of the frost and cold, when a great tree, its fibres made brittle by the continued freezing, would "jump its stump," break the saw, spin wildly and fall wide of the spot selected. Once I saw an enormous spruce do this and cast its ponderous length, bristling with splintered branches, across the backs of a team of horses, breaking their spines and reducing them to a shattered, screaming tangle of bloody flesh and crushed bone.

Men were hurt and some of them died of their injuries, but in spite of the fact that they were many miles from a doctor and their treatment was of the crudest, many of them chose to stay in camp and recover instead of making an attempt to get to civilization and a hospital. It was my job to administer first aid and make later dressings, and although I was squeamish about it at first, I got so I could swab out a hole quite handily.

I well remember coming in from a hunt at our camps at Burbank Operation down on the West Branch to find the red ruin of a man stretched out on the office floor. The tree he had been falling had brushed the top of a dry tamarack high above him and, watching his falling tree, he did not see the dry top coming straight down upon him. It struck him full on the head and shoulders, and there was a piece of branch an inch in diameter protruding from the junction of the neck and left shoulder. Another large splinter had passed down through the scalp at the top of his head, its sharp end embedded somewhere under his left ear. He was in terrible pain and frantic with fear, but I could do nothing to relieve him.

It was the last of November. The rivers and lakes were fast making ice, but they were still open and, by a great stroke of luck, the superintendent, Mr. Terril, showed up in camp while I was trying to clean up around the wounds a little and make the man more comfortable. Our camp was about a mile back from the West Branch of the Penobscot where I had a canoe cached, so we made a crude stretcher out of an old camp spread and two poles, got the man and his belongings onto it and carried him down to the river over the flinty, frozen ruts that passed for a tote road.

Now the man was heavy and the stretcher an awkward thing to carry. Since Mr. Terril was a very tall man whereas I was somewhat short, a great part of the weight slid down on me, increasing my labors and reducing me to a state of trembling exhaustion. There was no rest or a chance to get my breath. We got the injured man stretched out in the bottom of the canoe, after some difficulty, and shoved off. The super took the stern paddle, while I went on my shaking knees in the bow, and we bucked the current of that river, swollen by the fall rains until I was sure I was going to die before I could draw the next breath. The paddles iced and grew heavy; my hands froze and then burned. My shoulders ached until they finally grew stiff and numb, but that old man, passing sixty years, sat in the stern and drove his paddle in so that I could feel the canoe rise and lunge ahead at every stroke.

As I remember, it was nine miles against a strong current to the North East Carry landing, and it seemed as if at every other stroke of the paddles the man in the bottom of the canoe yelped and screamed like a mortally hurt dog. And above these screams would come a harsh, "Put your back into it, son. You want me to shove this load all alone?"

Mr. Terril had telephoned for a team to meet us at the carry, and after we had loaded the man into the wagon, he told me that he would see to shipping him downriver and I should return to camp at once. I was all in, soaking wet with sweat, but I weighted the bow of the canoe and rode the current back downriver. It was quite dark before I reached the landing and I overshot it by half a mile before I realized that I was well on my way to Chesuncook. The pole took the place of the paddle and by some miraculous stroke of luck I managed to work back to the landing without getting swamped. I beached the canoe in black darkness and then had to negotiate that mile of rocks, stumps, roots and frozen ruts before I could hit camp and supper.

The man had the timber removed from his carcass and was out of the hospital in about six weeks. Mr. Terril made it known that I was a "turrible poor hand with a paddle," but graciously admitted that perhaps some day, when I had got some meat on my bones and some heft to work with, I might amount to "sunthin'." I retaliated with the truthful statement that I had a very poor chance of gaining any flesh or putting on any heft as long as I was forced to eat the spoiled codfish and frozen potatoes that he furnished his camps, and there was a noticeable coolness between us thereafter.

I have no desire or intention to write a history of logging operations or to enter into the technicalities connected with them. This has already been done by more able and experienced men with a flair for research and I would not presume to compete with them. For some reason or other, it seemed as if I *had* to go north into the woods, and so I went. I was young and easily impressed and some of my recollections are very vivid. Many of my experiences were strange and enjoyable; others of the routine kind are half forgotten. I kept no records, took no photographs, and so, of course, remember only those things which seemed interesting or important to me when they took place.

The thunderous tumult of logs being sluiced through a dam like the one at Canada Falls or the stone structure on Sourdnahunk Stream is something not easily forgotten. The great wings of tangled timber at the roll dams on the West Branch above Five Islands, the shouts of the batteau-men, mingled with the crash of dynamite and the roar of swift water, will remain a thrilling memory as long as life itself. The feel of a twisting, pitching log beneath the feet of a novice and the final ability and skill to stay on and ride it out are a measure of accomplishment that defies description.

I worked in the winter logging camps and on dam and road construction jobs. The living conditions were usually very good on the summer construction work, but I liked the spring drives best of all.

There was always a sense of coming action on the drives, whether they were on some small rapid stream high in the hills or on the waters of the Penobscot and its larger branches. The swift motion and cheerful sound of running water brought a sense of joyful release from the drab, frozen, winter trails. Everyone seemed to step more freely, to be filled with vigor and at the same time relaxed. Men stalked about the driving wangans in new calked boots and stagged pants. Their battered felt hats assumed a more cocky angle, they practiced tricks with cantdogs, tried their skill on the logs, and every now and then there was a fight. The warm spring sun drew the sap up into the thawing trees and at the same time sent the sluggish blood more swiftly through the veins of men.

When two evenly matched drivers fought, it could be, and usually was, a brutal reversion to the primitive. They slugged each other with the intent to destroy utterly, using fists, heads and feet wherever they found it expedient, and they might bear the marks of such combat to their graves. These battles were not indulged in frequently, for their consequences were likely to be serious, and it often took months and years to pile up enough grievances to bring things to a head.

I witnessed one fight where the two gladiators fought, according to previous agreement, with fist and head only, for one hour and ten minutes by my watch. It is true that along toward the last of the affair the action slowed up, but for more than a half-hour they tried earnestly and viciously to punch or butt one another out of existence. During the next half-hour they panted, gasped, swung wildly without much damage to either one, and the last ten minutes were spent stretched out side by side on the ground where they threshed and rolled and made ineffectual and feeble swipes at each other. The two somewhat reluctantly agreed to call it a draw when they found it physically impossible to continue, but instead of calling off the feud, they stalked around for weeks eying each other speculatively and needing very little excuse or urging to try it again.

The so-called professional river drivers were a hard lot. There were a few farmers and downriver men who went down the rivers for a cash stake. They worked in the woods all winter, took on a short drive and then planned to be home for the spring plowing and planting. They were on the whole good, quiet, efficient workmen, solid Maine citizens as are found in all the small towns and villages. They earned their pay and saved their money, and they had little to do with the hell-raising gentry.

The younger men who followed the camps and rivers had just two thoughts in mind and just two topics of conversation—rum and women. You might hunt the world over and fail to find a breed to compare with them in sheer blasphemy, profanity, lechery and drunkenness. Every other spoken word was an oath or an obscenity, and most of them had a fund of anecdotes and foul ditties that they told or droned out in doubtful melody around the evening fires. Some of these are funny but unprintable, and the favorites are so obscene there is no point in them—no rhyme or anything else to appeal to one's sense of humor, just a mass of filthy words. I know from experience that when men are segregated far from the opposite sex their minds incline in that direction. They yearn for that which they have not, but never, in all my association with men and beasts, have I seen or heard anything to compare with some of the escapades and epics as related by these Lotharios of the fresh-water logans.

We had a man with us on Russell Stream one year who was noticeably worried. It seems that, after finishing up his winter's work, he went down to Bangor for a little rest and relaxation. After cleaning up he bought some liquor and repaired to a certain brothel well known to him. Later, after getting pretty well down into the bottle and having frolicked with one of the public ladies, he woke up in the night to find this houri going through his pants. Bounding from his couch, he grabbed the pants away from her and seizing them by the legs struck her across the face with them. She went down, kicked spasmodically a couple of times and then stretched herself out on the floor—as he put it, "deader than a hammer." Dumfounded that such an apparently healthy and rugged female should succumb to so trivial a blow, he stood aghast and then hurried into his clothes and flew out of there. It was not until some time and a pint later that he discovered that the crystal of his large silver railroad watch was broken and the mystery of the lady's sudden collapse explained. The watch, a piece of considerable weight and tightly enclosed in the watchpocket of the pants, must have smitten the victim

Ridge Runner

with considerable force somewhere around the temple. We never heard anything from the matter, the law stayed in its usual haunts below Moosehead, and we can only assume that the lady recovered.

"A man wasn't comfortable and couldn't feel settled until he got good and lousy." So the saying went.

I have seen three or four of these rugged individualists sitting on the deacon seats picking lice and crabs from the hair under their arms and comparing them as to size and viciousness. There would be long and sometimes quite humorous discussions as to whether the East or West Branch lice were more active and therefore more desirable. One man swore that he took three Great Northern lice over onto the Katahdin Pulp and Paper outfit, over in the East Branch country, and these kept the East Branchers off him all winter. He said there were some terrible lice fights that went on clear up into his head and whiskers, but the ones he brought with him repelled all boarders and all he had when he left in the spring were the same three. He knew they were the same ones because they had "G.N.P." stamped on their backs.

It was generally believed at this time that a youth could not rightly call himself a man until he had contracted a good case of gonorrhea, and there was no question as to the manly status of most of them. They were strong and they were tough and they had to be. A man must be practically indestructible in order to work up to his waist in icy water while suffering from an active venereal disease. They wrapped themselves in dirty rags and worked in the cold water all day, slept in their wet clothes all night on a thin padding of brush, and swore to God they would rather have it than a bad cold. They rolled her high wide and handsome until their late thirties when they would feel the first twinge of rheumatism. Their kidneys would begin to give difficulty, stomach trouble would make itself known and they would curse the cooks for putting saltpeter in the food.

The best of them drew soft jobs watching camps or tending gates on the dams, while the rest worked less and less and finally hung around the towns and cities doing the roughest kind of unskilled labor for as long as they could stand it and then going on the bum. A man could live after a fashion for quite a while on little or nothing, if his friends were generous. One would see these specimens now and again, hanging around the railroad station or the employment office, or engaged in some piece of construction work where they leaned heavily on a shovel or feebly swung a pick. Often I would see one of these half-crippled wrecks whom I had known when he was at the peak of his arrogance, and I could never pass him by without speaking. His gaunt face would light up—"By God, I didn't think you'd remember me. I was at Albert Hurley's wangan on Big Russell at Caribou Deadwater in 'sixteen where you was clerk, an' we had to haul the whole damned drive down to the dam against a head wind for forty days. I like to have broke my goddam' back windin' on them headworks—remember?" So I remembered and he remembered, until I had to move on about my business; and at the last he would mumble, not meeting my eye, "I been havin' kind of rough sleddin' "—and I would give him what change I could spare and sometimes more.

Once I walked the whole length of Exchange Street with a beautiful girl on my arm and at least a dozen times I had to stop and advance "a little loan." My applicants were rough and uncouth and they smelled of strong drink, but they greeted me with respect and affection and I could no more have refused them than I could the girl herself.

CHAPTER VI

JAMIE MCGASKIL had five hundred and forty dollars in cash and a heart brimming with good intentions. In addition, he had a pair of battered old calked boots and a stained old war bag with three pounds of spruce gum, two plugs of chewing tobacco, and four pairs of wool socks in it. These possessions, together with the tattered rags that covered his hard, stocky five foot eight inches of Scotch-Irish blood, bone, and muscle, were the entire results of ten years in the woods and on the drives. Jamie was twenty-six years old and for the last seven years had been conducting himself in such a way as to work up quite a reputation for hell-raising.

Yes, you could mention Jamie most anywhere from Bangor to Churchill Lake and someone would be sure to bring forth some new episode that would produce much hilarious back-slapping and shouts of appreciation. When Jamie frolicked, he went at it wholeheartedly, and when he fought, it was with a dour Scotch grimness that chilled the blood and took all the joy out of combat. He was liked and respected, and despite the broken jaws and black eyes that followed in the wake of one of his periodic sprees, he had but one real enemy—the bottle.

Jamie was a good man to work. He was good with the

axe, crosscut, or cantdog. He could drive team, roll landing, ride a log in quick or dead water and handle a batteau on the drives. He was always welcome in any wangan and could have worked steadily all year round, had he cared to. He could have saved his money and gone up in the world of logging, but after a few months in the timber, he would get restless—and then Bangor and the bottle.

This last year had been different. The urge had come many times, but for almost twelve months he had "hung her tough," going from fall and winter logging onto a spring drive and from thence to the long summer drive on the West Branch. It took quite a while to work up a stake at the winter wage of a dollar a day and found, but when driving pay starts at three and a half, the amount in the time book grows unbelievably.

And now with all the money in the world pinned safely inside his stag shirt with a huge blanket pin, he was on the train and bound downriver again. Same old dirty smoker, same old stinking, lolling, lecherous bunch of river hogs as in the years before—only this time it was going to be different. Everything was going to be different.

This time there would be no drinking, no foregathering with the filthy worn-out drabs that picked your pockets while you slept. No fighting, howling, glass-breaking, furniture-smashing period of insanity that ended in deathly sickness in some dirty back room, or in a cell next to the city police court.

Jamie let his head rest against the back of the seat and luxuriated in thoughts of virtue, while the train rolled and lurched through the bright August day.

First, he would go to the best clothing store in town and buy him a whole outfit straight through from underwear to a nice dark suit with shoes, socks, shirts, ties and a new hat. Then he would buy a new woods outfit for the coming winter and spring. Wool pants, heavy underclothes, mackinaw, shoepacs, and a real Stetson hat. He would buy only the very best of everything and have the things sent over to the Exchange Hotel where he would get a room with bath.

Then, after he had bathed and shaved, he would dress up in his new clothes and go down to the dining room and order the damnedest biggest steak that ever came off a steer—steak with great chunks of melted butter on it, and mashed potatoes and boiled onions and everything else that he or the waiter could think of that was good to eat. And after he had eaten all he could hold, he would light up a good ten-cent cigar and sit back in comfort, watching the crowds of less fortunate and less virtuous citizens passing up and down Exchange Street. Yes, he would sit there in the big comfortable leather chair and watch the life of the city through the clean plate glass windows of the hotel lobby, and after a while he would go to the Bijou, or perhaps the Opera House, and then a good night's sleep between clean, smooth sheets on a soft mattress instead of stinking blankets on a pile of lumpy hemlock bows.

And in the morning he would do the thing that he had vaguely planned for years. He would go home. He would get on the train again and go back to the tiny village in the hills and walk out to the rocky mountain farm that he had hated so; and with his fine new clothes and his roll of bills in his pocket, the folks would be glad to see him and they would all have a mild celebration. He would give the old man four hundred bucks to make up for his lost services, and all his relatives would make much of him.

He closed his eyes to conjure the scene more vividly and felt a heavy hand upon his shoulder.

Big Steve Ramsey was a successful operator. One of the old time company superintendents who could cut and drive millions of feet of timber cheaply and still feed and house his crews well enough so that men were anxious to work for him. He knew loggers and how to get the most work out of them, and he had had his eye on Jamie for a long time. He was big, and he was hearty and easy-going, but he had been a terrible fighter in his youth and young manhood and all men respected him.

It was a signal honor for an ordinary woodsman to be noticed by Steve to the extent of familiarity, and when he grinned cordially and demanded that Jamie shove over and give him room in the seat, McGaskil snapped out of his daydreams and hastily made room.

The big man lost no time. "They tell me," he began pleasantly, "that you made a long haul of it this time."

"I did that," answered Jamie, proudly. "I stuck her out a year lackin' a few days an', mister, I got a roll to prove it."

"And, I suppose," said Ramsey slyly, "that you plan to leave a trail of wreckage right through the heart of the city twenty-four hours after you hit town."

"That," said Jamie firmly, "is jest what I don't intend to do. I've had me fun an' I'm goin' to settle down an' save me money. I'm buyin' me a new outfit of clothes an' some woods gear, an' then off to the farm to see the folks for a few days before I ship out again."

Ramsey studied him thoughtfully for a moment. "Well," he said soberly, "you have a chance, but you've been at this hellery for some time. A red head, a hard fist, a quick temper and a love for the bottle is a hard combination to beat. Tell you what—I'm openin' up seven camps right away up in the Cuxabexis country. It will be quite a job to cut and drive the stuff, but if you want to keep reasonably sober and out of trouble this trip, I'll take you on as camp foreman at seventy-five a month for the cutting and five dollars a day on the drive. You think you can swing it? I'll be at the Bangor House for a week, so think it over and let me know when you are ready for the job."

For a long time after the superintendent had gone, Jamie sat staring straight ahead of him as though in a trance, and then he spoke aloud in wonder: "By the great red, roarin', searin', snappin' flames o' hell, all a man has to do is jest *think* about bein' decent, an' look what happens!"

It *might* be true that if Tobey Ash had not got on the train at Waterville, things would have turned out differently. Tobey was one of those legendary drunks who tried earnestly to kill himself with cheap alcohol as long as there was any money to buy it. All that saved his life from drunk to drunk was the fact that, three or four days after he hit civilization, he usually got rolled and from that time on until he shipped out he was flatly on the bum. They say that one time, when he nearly died from a bout with bootleg alcohol taken with a very little faucet water, the doctor told him positively that he would certainly die if he did not stop the session and sober up. Whereupon Tobey rose up, found a cheap undertaker, bought a coffin and made all the arrangements for his funeral. These final chores completed, he bought another half-gallon of alcohol, put it on a chair at the head of his bed and finished out his drunk in peace.

Tobey was an expert saw-filer and made considerable money during the winter months, sometimes working late into the spring, so he usually had ample funds to begin an epic bender, but lacked the head or stomach for a standing finish. He got onto the train at Waterville and he was certainly a mess. He had started for Bangor two days before, but becoming unbearably thirsty, had got off the train at the above-mentioned town where he knew of a sure source of supply. The stuff was home-distilled by the washboiler method and horrible both to the taste and stomach, but Tobey didn't mind. It was both quick and stunning in action and that was just what he needed. He came lurching up the aisle of the smoker peering to right and left through reddened eyes that were swollen nearly shut. There was a white rime at the corners of his mouth, he was filthy and he smelled, but he was gloriously drunk and he had the best part of a quart tucked up under the front of his old grey sweater.

And so Old Scratch himself in the person of drunken Tobey Ash came and sat down in the seat beside Jamie. And twice and thrice was the young man tempted and three times he refused, strong in the sense of his new-found pride. But the journey was long, the tempter wily and insistent, and at last to stop his maudlin beg-

ging, Jamie lifted the bottle and took a fair sup. The nauseous stuff burned down his throat, sour and gagging. His stomach heaved and almost refused it, but after a few seconds of suspense there was a little prickling burst of warmth and fire that spread blessedly and numbingly through blood and nerves and into the very bones. Jamie sighed and reached for his pipe while the sun grew magically brighter on the green fields flying by the windows, and even the smoky air of the dingy coach seemed to take on a new and invigorating freshness.

The second drink was larger and it went down much easier, and by the time the bottle was finished our hero had reached a state of benign magnificence, carefree and jovial. Not drunk, you understand, but uplifted to that plane where ordinary earthly troubles become too trivial even to think about. The hand is steady, the knees firm, and the eyes still clear and keen, but all the nagging doubts, the petty responsibilities dim and fade—and to hell with them!

It was in this beatific state of mind that Jamie McGaskil crossed the street in front of the Maine Central Station at Bangor, Maine, on a golden sunshiny day late in August of 1915. The sharp edges of his good intentions were turned slightly by the corrosiveness of his potations, but they were still with him, and with the purchase of new clothes in mind, he made his way up Exchange Street.

Bangor in 1915 was not the roistering, frolicking Queen that she had been in the heyday of big pine and heavy shipping, but she still sat on a throne of sorts and welcomed the weary and wayward with open arms and a sly smile. There were certain accommodations frowned on by Church and State alike, but the woodsmen came, they had money to spend, and hospitality of the kind they liked was due them. Their pleasures were short and violent and their stay was usually brief, so the city pulled aside its skirts, set its virtue among the elms on the high hills, thundered the wrath of God from its pulpits—and took in the cash through the dives in the dark back streets.

The hot sun beat pleasantly upon Jamie McGaskil's shoulders, while his ears rang with the unaccustomed clanging of trolley cars and the clop-clop of the horses' feet upon the pavements. The air was foul with the reek of coal smoke, the effluvia of frying onions from an outdoor hotdog stand, and the strong smell of hot asphalt. The open doors of cheap restaurants and drugstores sent forth their own thick, indescribable odors to mingle with those of the street, and his heart lifted with a sense of reckless freedom and well-being, as his sharpened senses greedily absorbed the scents and sounds of the city.

The store which he had in mind was well up toward the end of the street, but little more than halfway to his objective he ran into one of those traps set for the unwary or slightly intoxicated woodsman—one of those temporary establishments that may last a month or perhaps six. It may move during that time from one street or one city to another, because it would not be safe or profitable to stay in one location very long. This particular clothing "emporium" was in dire straits, as great red-lettered signs proclaimed. Its lease was up. It was necessary to move at once, and its entire stock of choice men's clothing, as well as other valuable merchandise, must be sold at a terrific loss in order to meet this cruel emergency.

Now Jamie had no intention of patronizing this establishment, but the glaring signs smote upon his eyeballs and slowed his steps. There was a dummy in the window fully dressed in a blue serge suit with white pipings on the vest. He stopped, hesitated and was lost, for the proprietor was an aggressive individual who pounced upon opportunity long before it knocked on his door. A firm hand closed upon Jamie's upper arm, there was a sudden flurry of words and action, and he found himself inside the dark, musty interior of the store.

He cursed, he struggled, he expostulated and even threatened his ravisher with bodily injury, but in the end he succumbed. He bought the blue serge suit with the white pipings on the vest, yellow shoes, socks, shirts —one of them a bright blue in color—a red and yellow tie, and a sailor hat of rough straw with a blue and yellow band around it. Every article was positively guaranteed not to stretch, shrink, or ravel at the edges. He changed into his new outfit in a dirty little toilet at the back of the shop and strode forth in glory into the warm afternoon sunshine.

Jamie was quite a sight.

And while he was being sold into sartorial splendor, the word had gone forth. Tobey Ash began it with the statement that Jamie was in town with a thousand dollars to get rid of within a week's time. Down at the employment office where the clan, already broke and ready to ship out, congregated, cadging a dollar now and then for a drink or a meal, it was whispered, "Jamie McGaskil's in town with a most ungodly roll." The hangers-on over at the Adams House heard it and passed it along to various secret haunts. The proprietors of certain illegal but wide-open establishments got the word and, with mingled sensations of cupidity and unease, passed the news along to others of their ilk. A great many people in various walks of life began to yearn for the pleasure of Jamie's company and a look at his bank roll.

It would be inadvisable as well as practically impossible to follow Mr. McGaskil's wavering trail from the clothing store at two p.m. on that memorable day to the time that he awoke beneath a screen of shrubbery surrounding a spacious estate some distance from the heart of the city. We may assume that he had eaten and partaken of liquid refreshment among friends, for when he awoke it was with the certain knowledge that he had slept long and heavily with his mouth wide open. The dryness of his mouth and throat bore testimony to the fact and, as he groaned and stirred upon his hard bed, the fact became also apparent that he was very wet. The state of the grass and hedge that sheltered him indicated that he had slumbered through a heavy shower, and his new clothes clung clammily to his shivering frame. With shaking fingers he fumbled through his pockets and after a fearful search discovered considerable sums of money well distributed throughout his clothing. His spirits lifted a little. He had been among friends anyway and hadn't been rolled, so he lurched to his feet and set off for a familiar haven of refuge and refreshment not too far away.

Some two hours later the inner man had become strengthened and restored, but the outer trappings were fast becoming the source of much hilarity and ribald comment. That seventy-five dollar suit was shrinking visibly. One could almost see the legs of the trousers contracting and the sleeves of the coat creeping up the limbs which they were supposed to cover, and with each fraction of an inch of their shrinking Jamie McGaskil's wrath grew and demanded outlet. No man, especially a fighting man, likes to be made an object of ridicule in the eyes of his fellows. Righteous indignation lends even greater strength to the mightiest arm, and on his way back to the clothing store for an accounting Jamie acquired a considerable following who were interested in human rights—and the survival of the fittest.

The unlucky Levantine chose to get tough about the affair. He not only refused flatly to consider any adjustment, but chose to assume a facetious attitude toward the transaction. That was a grave error.

Jamie hooked a left to the soft belly, following it with a swinging right to the cheekbone. The proprietor sat down heavily, crossed his eyes, uncrossed them and then began to squeal like a stuck hog and a paunched bear combined. The audience cheered wildly. Jamie glowered and blew on his knuckles—and then came the police.

Court was in session.
The complainant, his face fast assuming the hue of long kept beef, and his assailant stood before the bar of justice and even the stern face of the law could scarce

forbear a smile. That suit was still shrinking. The sleeves of the coat were nearly to Jamie's elbows and the legs of the trousers were more than halfway up to his knees.

After reading the warrant charging Mr. McGaskil with assault upon the person of one Benjamin Feinberg, the judge gazed sternly upon both culprit and complainant. "Either of you represented by counsel? No. Well, possibly you are both familiar with the procedure in such cases. What say you to the charge as read, Mr. McGaskil? Are you guilty or not guilty?"

Jamie drew a long breath. He still had money and could pay quite a stiff fine.

"Guilty, yer honor," he said firmly, "but I think I had good reason for the offence. Look at this suit, yer honor. Look at this suit for which I paid yon blackhearted sheeney seventy-five dollars in good hard-earned cash only yesterday."

"You will forbear the calling of hard names in this court, young man," said the judge sternly, "or else be found in contempt."

"Your honor," whimpered Mr. Feinberg, "look at my face."

"Well," said the judge sourly, "I've looked at it and I don't like it, so speak when you're spoken to." He pondered a moment. "Well, I fail to see any reason for dragging this out. Since you plead guilty, Mr. McGaskil, I hereby fine you ten dollars, together with the costs of court amounting to four eighty-five. Pay the clerk, please, or go to jail for ten days."

Jamie stood somewhat bewildered by the lightness

of the sentence. Mr. Feinberg stood just within reach on his left and the arresting officer on his right.

"Fourteen dollars and eighty-five cents," Jamie muttered softly and, fishing a roll of bills from his pocket, he put a ten and a five dollar bill on the table before him. And then beside that contribution he carefully placed a second fifteen dollars, replaced his money in his pocket and, while court and spectators stood aghast, his left hand shot out, spun the store proprietor around to face him whilst his good right fist shot out in a straight overhand punch that landed flush on Mr. Feinberg's prominent and fleshy nose.

The sound of the blow cracked wickedly through the silent room. It had a sickening, meaty sound of finality. The seller of shoddy suits clapped both hands over his ruined face, sat down upon the courtroom floor and made bubbly noises through his fingers.

"Yer honor," said Jamie with dignity, " 'tis paid for in advance and cheap at the price."

"Yes," said the judge, quietly, " 'tis as you say, cheap at the price, but now there is a little matter of say fifty dollars for contempt of court. Will you pay, Mr. McGaskil, or go to jail for sixty days?"

"I'll pay," said Jamie, "but, yer honor, I'll have ye know I have no contempt fer yerself or this court. 'Tis a true place of justice, as all men now know."

And that is how a certain river driver and brush jumper of the old days attained near-immortality. His name is not as written here, but there are men living who knew him and have heard the tale, and they will unhesitatingly vouch for the truth of it. The man whom

I have named Jamie McGaskil never became a foreman at seventy-five dollars a month. He worked less and less every year, and finally met his death in a burning shack where he lay stupefied with drink, an empty bottle in his hand.

CHAPTER VII

It could be taken for granted that most of the Maine and Canadian woodsmen were pretty handy with edged tools, but if an expert piece of adzing or hewing was required, the work was invariably done by one of the older men. There were usually one or more of these skilled workers in wood or iron to be found in a crew, their backs a little bent, their whiskers turning white, but strong and hearty in spite of advancing age. They had learned to be temperate before it was too late, or were possessed of magnificent constitutions that dissipation could not break. Some of them had saved a little money and acquired small farms to which they would retire when they became unable to work for wages. They were slow moving but industrious and many of them were blessed with the quiet, dry sense of humor that is commonly attributed to the Maine Yankee. Listening to them talk among themselves, one could glean a fair knowledge of what went on in the woods when things were *really* rough, and sometimes when they knew I was listening they would spin some yarn that was unforgettable in its sly humor.

I remember one warm spring day at Seboomook Dam when I sat with two of these ancients on the great log structure, soaking up the sun and listening to the roar of the falls below us. I was drowsily content and only half listening to the lazy drone of their voices as they smoked and spat, when I heard a name mentioned that was familiar to me.

"Yes," said one of them, "Simmy is an able man—good man to have around, but he has them spells when he gets so damned lazy it's jest plain aggravatin'."

Now I knew very well this man of whom they spoke, and he was famous far and wide for his feats of strength and his ability to do a prodigious amount of work.

"Well," said the second greybeard, "that's the first time I ever heard anyone say *that* man was lazy. Worked with him man and boy for thutty-five years an' never knew him to shirk a lift or drop a load. Got considerable of a reputation, Simmy has, good reputation, too."

Simmy's disparager puffed strongly on his reeking pipe and spat disdainfully down into the water:

"Hell, I ain't sayin' he ain't a good man to work. All I know is what I see. Back in the old pod-auger days him an' me come up from Ross Farm to North East Carry with a batteau load of stuff to carry across to the West Branch. We unloaded an' after we had et an' had a smoke, I roped up some plunder, horsed her onto my back an' lit out, leavin' him to foller. I had a pretty fair load an' when I got to the halfway mark, I eased up against a stump to take the weight off my back a little, an' then I seen him comin'. Damned if I could hardly believe my eyes. You know what that buzzard had for a load? Well, sir, there he come a-strollin' along an' all he had was a bar'l o' pork an' a new grindstone."

Considering the weight of a full barrel of pork and a grindstone, I wondered just what might constitute a "fair load." Possibly three or four bales of hay surmounted by a cookstove. But I kept quiet and asked no questions.

It was at Cuxabexis in 1916 that I heard the story of Esau Kant. This is not his real name and I will not name the man who told me the story, for he was frankly reluctant, somewhat superstitious, and swore by the Holy Old Mackinaw that the facts as he told them were as true as the Bible.

This man Esau Kant, as we shall call him, came into our office at Cuxabexis Depot on an evening late in December. It was a foul day, with a northeast blizzard blowing up, and it was all the tote team could do to get through from Chesuncook Dam even with half a load. He rode in on the sled and, after I had checked the load, I found him in the office, huddled close to the stove—a great bear of a man in a heavy fur coat with half the hair gone from it and a greasy fur cap that came well down over his ears and neck. I went straight to my desk, but noticed that, although the foreman, the blacksmith, and one of the straw bosses were in the room, all conversation had ceased. The big ram-down stove was red-hot all along its sides and the old fur coat began to steam and stink like a wet dog.

I turned and snapped irritably, "Oh, for God's sake, skin yourself out of that hide or get away from the stove, and take off that damned cap before you melt. Who are you, anyway, and what do you want?"

He moved away from the stove and out into the light. A great paw went up and pulled off the cap, and then I knew who he was. I'd heard of him before. His face and head were as smoothly pink as a freshly scraped hog. There were no eyebrows or lashes, no sign of a whisker or suspicion of hair anywhere on his head.

"Name o' Kant," he squeaked in a thin, reedy voice, "Esau Kant. Goin' through to Number Seven on comp'ny business an' need grub an' a bed for the night."

He turned to Tom McLean, the boss. "Where shall I sleep, Mr. McLean?"

Tom stood up and answered shortly, "The clerk here will give you blankets and spreads from the storehouse, and you can break open a bale of hay and bed down in the horse hovel. It will be warm enough there and cook will feed you after the crew has eaten. You lousy, Mr. Kant?"

Esau stated in that whispery treble that he was just from downriver and clean, so I went out and found clean bedding for him.

The thing bothered me. I had heard rumors about the man, that he was entirely hairless and that he spread bad luck wherever he was allowed to stay for any length of time. This cold reception of a traveler on a stormy night was quite new and strange to me, and the more I thought about it the more consumed with curiosity I became.

Tom McClean would tell me nothing except that Kant worked out of the office at Bangor and that no crew would have anything to do with him. He claimed that was all he knew and refused to discuss the matter.

Later on, one evening when he was in an especially expansive mood, he said more: "There's several old-timers in the woods that know all about Esau and how he lost his hair. They are few and getting pretty old.

and they are widely scattered, but I'll tell you this much —if you can get Rocky Emmons, the old hair-pounder that's doing our toting in from Chesuncook, alone sometime and get him half drunk, he might tell you all about it. They say he was in camp with Esau when it happened and is the only one around these parts that will speak civilly to him. They say Esau Kant is older than God and Rocky is older than Esau. Anyway there is some kind of a bond between them because Rocky gives him rides and will even eat with the bald-headed old bastard. Won't none of these other men sleep under the same roof with him, but none of them know why."

Sometimes for no reason at all things will break right. The day before Christmas, McLean, the head clerk, a couple of straw bosses and the feeder took off down to Duck Lake and across to Chesuncook village for a Christmas celebration. Because I was not particularly keen about going and someone had to be there to look after things, I wished them well and prepared to write a lot of letters that evening. Along about eight o'clock, Mrs. Gunn at Chesuncook Dam called me on the phone, moved her small phonograph up near her telephone and played some Christmas carols for me. After that she put on a brand new record, "There's a little bit of bad in every good little girl," and closed the concert with the "Humoresque." The music made me restless and lonesome. I tried to write, but with little success, so I stoked the stove and wandered around the room, feeling pretty low in spirits. I sat down at the head clerk's desk toying with the idea of calling the pretty red-headed operator at the Grant Farm just to exchange Christmas greetings, and then I happened to glance down under the clerk's bunk and my heart gave a leap. I saw the end of a shoe box covered with torn wrapping paper. I knew well enough what was in it—a quart of cheap whiskey mailed in to a man who had settled up and left camp weeks ago.

Liquor was forbidden in the camps, but here it was —and Rocky Emmons had pulled into camp with a load of freight this very day.

I remember how bright the stars shone in the still, cold night and how the smoke from the pipe in the men's camp and cook house rose up thin and white against the stars that Christmas Eve. Rocky was in the blacksmith's shop yarning with the blacksmith and the filer, and he was decidedly grumpy when I told him his load was short a few items and that I wanted to check with him.

We went back through the snapping frost over the dry, creaking snow in the camp yard and into the warm office where I sat him down in our most comfortable chair and, instead of the hated transfer slips, I brought forth the bottle and two tin cups.

I said, "It's Christmas Eve, Rocky, and me here alone. I have heard that you are a man of proper discretion, with a sufficient capacity for hard liquor. So drink hearty to this night and the day to come."

He was a small dried-out little man with a wizened face burned and seasoned by many frosts and suns. A face, old, wise and somehow a little sorrowful in repose. There was a look of mingled surprise and delight upon it as he took the bottle and poured himself a generous drink.

I said, "I'll drink with you, but I'll have to nurse it

along. I have the heart of a man, but the stomach of a boy, and the damned stuff makes me sick."

We touched cups and drank, and I set the bottle near him, locked the door and blew out all the lamps but one.

His guts must have been galvanized and copper-plated because the bottle was nearly half gone before he showed signs of a drink. He talked, yes, but very rationally of places *I* had been and people *I* had known, and only when I had nearly despaired did he begin to go back into the past. I watched him like a cat at a rathole and then, with a touch of genius entirely foreign to my nature, with the bottle still a little less than half full, I yawned and announced drearily that it was time for sleep. He peered at me with a comical look of consternation. "Good God, clerk, bed, an' the bottle only half gone? Put another slug into you an' sit down."

I muttered crossly that the stuff would only make me more sleepy and to hell with it.

I picked up the bottle and cups, while his eyes anxiously followed my every move, and then I hesitated and appeared to ponder. I said, "Tell you what. You finish the bottle and tell me a certain tale that I will name, and by that time it will be Christmas morn. Will you do that?"

He looked longingly at the bottle and I passed it to him along with his cup.

"You're a good lad," he said quietly, "but not so sly as ye think. I know well what it is that ye would know. Ye have been here an' there and 'round about, an' men speak well of ye; so sit ye down, me boy, an' I'll tell ye of Old Esau. *But* ye must promise me on this Holy Eve that ye will not bandy the tale about or repeat it to any man whilst Esau lives amongst us."

He drank deeply, wiped his mouth on the back of his hand, touched a match to the bowl of his foul old pipe and settled himself in his chair. Now, before I relate the story almost exactly as it was told to me, and this I am able to do because I wrote it down at its ending, I must digress a bit. Esau's downfall was caused by a small bird and, since this bird is one of the principals in the tale, it is necessary to speak a little of the Canada Jay, or—as it was commonly called by the woodsmen— the gorbie or moose bird.

Years ago, when I first went into the woods north of Moosehead, these birds were very plentiful and very tame and fearless. Lunching alone on the trail, I have had them fly down and take crumbs from my fingers a number of times. Wherever there was food or a camp ground, there was sure to be a flock of the sooty-grey little thieves hanging around and nobody ever thought of harming them until in later years the sports found them easy targets for their twenty-twos. It was commonly believed among the older men that it was exceedingly bad luck for anyone to offer them harm or to drive them away, in spite of the fact that I have seen them around wangans and open camps so thick that they became a real nuisance. Margarine especially attracted them, and many times I have seen them swoop down and scoop a beakful from right under the noses of a feeding crew seated at an outdoor table. Sometimes when a man was recovering from a big drunk and hanging on the edge of the D.T.'s, this could be very disconcerting, but the ordinary run of oldtimers took it as a matter of course. The gorbies are not nearly as numerous these days, and it has been a long while since I have seen one.

Rocky Emmons told the story fully, and this is the way of it:

"In the old days, an' I will not say how long gone it was, Esau was a bold giant of a man. He took charge in the camps an' on the drives, an' a hard man he was on a crew. His temper was quick an' his hand heavy an' he would take no lip from no man great or small. He had a thick head of yeller hair an' a great silky beard of the same, an' he spent hours combin' both the beard and his head till they would glisten an' gleam like yeller gold. There was a great mat of hair upon his chest an' it was thick, too, upon his arms and legs, an' he was sinfully proud of it all. This hair was a sign to him of his strength an' manhood an', bein' who an' what he was, no man made light of it twice. He was a cruel man with the might of an ox an' the heart of a weasel. No man called him 'friend,' but he could drive a crew an' get out the timber.

" 'Twas in a camp on the north side of Pogy Mountain on a day in January that the thing happened—a day of bitter cold an' drivin' snow, dry ice that could peel the hide from a man's face. Esau was wild because the crew laid in an' he spent half the day goddamning them all for a bunch of old women, even though he knew no man, exceptin' perhaps himself, could live an' work outside the way it was. After the noon meal, he calmed down some and sat in a great chair he had made for himself an' began to comb his hair an' beard. Most of the men was tired an' napped, but Jean Ayette from across the line, meself an' two others got out a deck of cards, but it was too cold to play. The wind shrieked an' howled over an' around the roof, drivin' the dry snow in through the chinkin', an' every once in a while you could hear one of the cedar roof shakes loosen up and clatter. Half the time the stove wouldn't draw an' would puke great puffs of smoke an' ashes out into the room. It was one cruel, God-awful day, boy, the like of which I have never seen since.

"It must have been around two o'clock when the storm was at its worst that the bird come—the little half-froze gorbie. He come an' fluttered his wings ag'inst the winder an' the wind caught him an' blew him away like a wisp of paper. An' then in the space of a few breaths he was back ag'in, an' Esau looked up an' seen him there flutterin' an' beatin' his wings ag'inst the pane. The bird dropped to the sill an' huddled into the corner where the frame was let into the logs, an' Esau got onto his feet an' stepped quick as a cat to the winder.

"He pulled the pegs that held in the frame an' scooped up the bird in his fist, yellin' for one of us to put the winder back in. Jean an' me put it back an' Esau sat down by the stove. The little grey head, lookin' this way an' that, peeked up through his fist an' the comical black-rimmed beady eyes never so much as blinked. He held the bird up level with his eye an' talked soft an' easy to it.

" 'Ha,' he says, 'ye have a familiar look about ye, me little grey crow. Ye look like Frenchy Aucoin with them two black eyes I gave him over on Black Brook two years gone, but Frenchy slipped on a jam an' went to hell.'

"He held the bird up closer an' looked an' looked, an' the bird looked back.

"'Now,' Esau went on, 'they's some that believe men has souls an', when they die, the souls come back an' flitter around. You wouldn't be the little thievin' flutterin' soul of Frenchy Aucoin, would ye, now?'

"The bird turned his head this way and that an' then he pulled back his little neck an' gave a tiny peck at the hand that held him.

"'Well now,' croons Esau, soft an' easy, 'well now, will ye look at that! I take him in and warm him in me own soft hands an' he bites me. Right before me own crew in me own camp the little grey crumb of a thievin' bastard of a crow bites me! Well, me fine rooster, if ye don't like it here, back ye go outside where ye belong. But first, before ye become overheated, leave us take off a few clothes.'

"An' then, whilst the whole caboodle of us stood by in shame an' fear, he opened his fist, spread an' clamped fast a wing with his thumb an' held the other open with a finger and, quick an' dainty as you please, he began to pluck the soft, short breast an' body feathers. The camp was deathly still, barrin' the howlin' o' the wind an' we could all hear the small rip-rip as the feathers came free. The gorbie squeaked once, an' then ag'in, an' was quiet.

"'Twas but a minute he worked, for he was quick with his hands, an' then he let out a beller of laughter an' held up the bird by the tips of his two wings. Ah, me lad, 'twas a pitiful sight, all the feathers stripped clean from the body an' only the wing an' tail feathers left. Even the neck he had picked, but the little black eyes were bright an' glitterin' an', whilst we looked, the head turned an' dipped an' the small beak plucked at his fingers.

"'An' now,' said Esau, an' there was the very devil in the tone of his voice, 'an' now, me little naked chicken, nobody asked ye here. Ye have been warmed an' entertained an' be damned to ye. Should ye turn out to be the black-eyed soul of Mister Aucoin, ye'll flutter back to hell an' be warm enough. An' if ye should be jest the little thievin' jay-bird I think ye are, then ye'll freeze quick an' easy, so out ye go.'

"He folded the bird's wings close to its body, closed his fist around it, an' steppin' to the winder, he loosed the sash an' thrust forth the naked bird into the storm. It turned once an' spread itself ag'inst the glass like one crucified an' then the wind whisked it away."

The old teamster paused for refreshment. His voice had taken on a slight burr, and his suspicion of a brogue was growing by the minute.

"There was little sleep amongst us that night," he went on. "We ate an' stretched on our bunks. Them was the days when we slept ten or a dozen under one long spread, an' when one turned in the night, all must do the same. The storm grew worse toward dark an' it tore at the camp until we thought surely the roof would leave her. Along towards mornin' the wind died an' we dozed off an' woke again when the bull-cook stoked the stove an' lit the lanterns. I was half asleep when he rolled us out an' was rubbin' the sleep from me eyes an' gropin' for me stags, when I heard the noise—a queer sound it was, a kind of a cross between a bleat an' a groan. It came from over in the corner where the wooden sink an' the water barrel stood, but before I could turn meself for a look, there was a gabble of French an' I seen Ayette down on his knees crossin' hisself whilst others of the crew stood starin' an' stiff with fear.

" 'Twas Esau's habit—to toughen him, as he said—to strip naked in the morn an' splash the icy water over his head an' chest, an' there he stood in the corner by the sink, white an' naked an', by the Little Old White-Eye an' the Holy Old Mackinaw, there was no wisp of hair upon him at any place! The thick mane of hair, the glossy beard, his brows an' even his eye-winkers was gone. The hair from his body was gone, too, an' he stood, scared an' shiverin', as white an' smooth as one of them marble statues of a man.

"The place was like a madhouse. The Frenchman Ayette was half mad with fear, an' Neil Hart, a Black Irishman with a tongue sharp as a new file, cursed Esau, the mother that bore him, the man that fathered him and that man's father before him. Up an' down an' over an' under an' before an' behind he cursed Esau, until the Irishman's eyes rolled in his head, the froth came from his mouth an' we could no longer understand his gibberish. An' Esau did nothin' but stand there in his nakedness an' tremble, an' it come to us that with his hair the best or the worst of him was gone with it, an' after a time we covered his shame with his clothes, hung his turkey on his shoulders an' druv him out from among us with kicks an' blows.

"The storm had stopped an' he went flounderin' off down the mountain through the deep snow. No man knows where he went, but for a matter of two years he was seen by none of us. 'Twas agreed that we would not speak of the thing, but the Frenchman Ayette could not hold his tongue and Hart had a loose mouth while in his cups. The tale went round, but 'twas told so many different ways an' so wildly that there seemed no truth to it at all, an' as those that were there at the camp on Pogy were killed off or died in their beds, the truth of the matter was lost entirely.

"They say that the Big Feller heard the tale an', believin' in neither good luck or bad, put Esau on the office payroll as a hunter of stray horses, an' when ye see him now, he is at that work. He travels when an' where he pleases, an' he tells me sunthin' drives him from place to place. There is no rest anywheres for him, for men refuse to sit at table with him or sleep under the same roof. He comes an' he goes, an' if ye make note of it, ye'll see that the storms come with him. As for me I can take no harm from him, for no worse luck can come upon me than I have already borne."

Rocky tipped the bottle and let the last drops run out. He raised the cup, swallowed quickly, and shook his head to clear it. He pulled out a great silver watch and peered at it owlishly. "It's now one o'clock of a Christmas morning, me bold, bouncin' broth of a penpusher. A very merry Christmas to ye, an' a happy New Year, an' a noisy Fourth. I have sat here yarnin' until there is a stiffness in me joints an', for some reason or other, a slight ringin' in me ears an' a dizziness in me head. 'Tis time for me to hit me bunk with perhaps your kind assistance, an' before I go, I must warn ye that when in liquor I am the most gorgeous, umbrageous damned liar that ever wagged a whiskey-loosened tongue. So pay no heed to my maudlin tales for there is no word of truth in them."

He sighed deeply and his chin dropped upon his chest.

He slept.

I saw and talked briefly with Esau Kant once more before he died. It was on a beautiful spring morning in early May. The air was soft and scented and the sun warm upon my back. I stopped on Kenduskeag Bridge in Bangor to watch a tiny raft of logs being towed down the stream by a skiff with a kicker on it. It was a very small raft, indeed scarcely larger than the floor of a good-sized room, but the breeze lifted a whiff of crushed wet spruce bark to my nostrils through the stink of the outboard, and a wave of nostalgia swept over me. In a few moments an elevator would shoot me up six floors to the company offices where, amidst clacking typewriters and adding machines, I would sit all day checking inventories and making marks in books.

Somebody stopped beside me. I had heard no sound of feet on the sidewalk, but I sensed that somebody was there—some curious city dweller, I thought. And then my nose was filled with the strong indescribable odor of the woodsman—spruce, hemlock, the softwood smell. Smoke, wood-smoke, lots of it. Sweat, tobacco and damp wool all combined and blended into one stout effluvium, tantalizing, masculine and wholly unforgettable.

A thin, reedy whisper, timid, hesitant, familiar:

"Quite a drive, mister."

I turned quickly and there he was towering above

me. His face was different, shrunken under the cheekbones and its pinkness changed to an unhealthy, greyish color. An old checked mackinaw hung loosely from his stooped shoulders, and one could see at a glance that not much solid flesh remained on the great frame. An old cloth cap was pulled well down upon his head, its visor half concealing the hairless brows and eyelids.

He looked hard at me for a moment and then turned his head aside.

"You left the woods, mister?"

I pointed to the row of windows high above us and answered shortly, "Up there."

He said slowly in that peculiar, piping voice, "I know you, mister, but where was it I seen you last?"

"Cuxabexis Depot, 1916," I answered.

"Yes," he said, "I remember."

He stirred uneasily and shifted his enormous feet in their broken shoepacs, waiting for the rebuff, I suppose. The raft had gone under the bridge and down the stream.

He half smiled and pointed with a warped thumb up the stream.

"Where's the rear, Jack?"

And I gave him the time-honored answer, "The rear's at the Old Pine Stump an' she looks like a hung drive."

One of my numerous bosses, a third or fourth assistant chief accountant, came by, nodded to me and sniffed at Esau with obvious disdain.

I put my hand in my pocket and said, "Well, Mr. Kant, I have to go to work, I suppose. Take it easy and I'll see you around. Are you broke?"

He looked at me with the saddest look I ever saw on

a human face. His throat worked and tears came into his eyes. Finally the words came and I heard that thin, reedy whisper for the last time: "No, mister, I ain't broke. I got enough—I got enough of *everything* now to see me through."

The boss said, "Who was that disreputable old rack of bones you were talking to down on the bridge?" And when I answered somewhat shortly that the gentleman's name was Esau Kant, he exclaimed, "Good God, you mean to tell me that there actually *is* such a person? I thought he was one of those legends like Paul Bunyan."

A few days later I learned that he had indeed become a legend—not a very well-known one, but a legend nevertheless. He died quietly and alone in a cheap lodging house and the Big Feller paid for his funeral.

CHAPTER VIII

I DREW my pay for performing certain tasks that had to do with speedily and efficiently turning the growing forests into such shape that they could be converted into newsprint, but a good part of my time was spent ramming around in the woods and getting lost.

The first few times I failed to show up at camp until sometime the next day, my associates were alarmed, built fires, shot off all my cartridges and in various other ways showed a flattering interest in my welfare wholly out of proportion to my importance. But when they found that my goings and comings were becoming unpredictable and that I refused to show any ill effects from my nocturnal absences, the whole situation developed into more or less of a joke. I even received a letter from my superiors advising that I hang a cowbell around my neck as a means of keeping in touch with the camp personnel. It was once suggested that if I spent a little more time on my paper work and less roaming around in the timber, I might get along faster.

Now I am well acquainted with the opinion that good woodsmen are not supposed to get lost, but I have yet to see one who has cruised strange country without map or compass who hasn't become slightly confused and as a result wasted considerable time and effort before re-

Ridge Runner

turning to the place from which he started—that is, if one is inclined to be truthful in such matters. I know there are those who claim they have never been lost, but if this is so, it is only because they have never been anywhere.

The difficulty does not lie in getting lost, but in the lack of ability to un-lose oneself before actual harm occurs and before it is too late. While I was with the Great Northern, I had a good country to get lost in. The river bounded it on the south, and I could travel straight north a couple of hundred miles through sheer wilderness in case I got real ambitious and chose to take that course. Thirty miles or so east would bring me into the Chesuncook Lake region, and I was pretty well hemmed in on the west by Russell Stream and Seboomook Lake. Both those localities were inhabited after a fashion, so I never went in that direction, for I had been there and found the country and few inhabitants both flat and uninteresting. I did most of my wandering where there was plenty of room and where I stood some chance of seeing something new once in a while.

Having been classified as an expert at getting lost by men who know a real expert when they see one, I will say that the quickest and easiest way to begin this delightful pastime is to keep one's nose and eyes close to the ground on something very enticing like a fresh deer or moose track. Follow it blindly and tenaciously, neglecting to notice any landmarks such as boulders, extra tall trees, distant mountains or exposed ridges, and along about dusk you will suddenly wake up to the fact that you have no idea where you are. You are lost!

If you are an average person of reasonable mental

stability and in fair physical shape, you will probably even so accept this fact with considerable uneasiness, but the worst you can experience, providing you keep quiet, is a night of discomfort. That is, providing you have matches and a heavy knife or belt axe. Before total darkness falls you should be safe, if not entirely comfortable, with some kind of a brush windbreak at your back and a fire at your feet.

Rain and snow can complicate matters a whole lot, but the fire will offset either of them to a certain extent. If you are a member of some hunting party, you can stay right there by your fire, pile on wood and softwood brush and let the smoke roll up. This will enable the other boys to do the walking, and you can save a lot of strength and energy by letting them find you and bring food. If you want to waste a few shells, shooting off your rifle now and then, it may help them locate you the sooner.

The way to kill yourself or mark yourself permanently with a fear of the woods is to let panic take over and drive you scrambling and threshing off into the dark, stumbling over blow-downs, floundering through swamps and wet places, shooting off all your shells within the space of a few minutes, and using up matches in an attempt to gain light. By daybreak your body will be exhausted and your brain will be incapable of intelligent reasoning, the sun will rise in the west, water will run up hill and hell will be to pay. Unless Lady Luck lays her hand upon your shoulder, you are in for a large dose of serious trouble.

One evening late in September, the camp foreman, a man who had spent nearly fifty years in the woods, told me of an outfit that had cut pine behind our choppings 'way back in the days when they were logging for masts and spars. He said these people came from Greenville, hauled in their supplies by ox team and built camps back on a ridge three miles or so from the river one at a time with teams of as many as two dozen head of cattle to a hitch. The foreman had seen no maps of the country, but he had been on a long horseback * north of the flat land where we were cutting and thought the remains of the old camps could still be found on the high ground somewhere along that ridge.

The next day I cleaned up my office work in the morning, and right after noon lunch took my rifle, made sure I had some matches, cigarette papers and tobacco, and struck off due north to find that ridge. They measured miles by running a deer to death up in that country, but I was on the high ground in a couple of hours and in a very short time thereafter I had found the old camp and the hovels for sheltering the oxen. The roof and rafters had fallen in, the old logs were crumbling, but there was enough left of the ancient structure to make it very interesting to me and I was quite excited over my discovery. I found a number of enormous pine stumps, most of them rotted and fallen into a rusty mound, but there were several in such a good state of preservation that one could plainly see that the growing trees must have been tremendous, both in length and girth.

It must have been shortly after three in the afternoon when I finally decided to return to camp and, reasoning

---

*A horseback (or hogback) in Maine parlance means a low narrow ridge that drops sharply to either side.

Ridge Runner

that if the ridge ran east and west as it surely did, I could cruise along it toward the east for a mile or so, swing south and then either hit the river or our cut-over area. In this way I could cover ground that I had not been over before and lay out a section for future hunting. I knew most of the deer were still on low ground and this ridge must touch the north end of a big cedar swamp east of our camp. I wanted to establish this meeting place and fix the point in my mind.

I hadn't gone far when I jumped the moose. I was far above him when he went out of a hemlock thicket making more noise than a freight car being shunted onto a siding. Now, I wasn't thinking of moose and didn't have any use for one at the moment. There was absolutely no reason for me to slip down the ridge, pick up the trail and go off on it like a starved wolf. I did just that, however, and a merry chase he led me! He went south into a swamp, swung back through it to high ground again where it was quite dry and the tracking sufficiently difficult to demand my entire attention in places. We left the extreme east end of the ridge, going straight downhill and I thought we were headed south toward the river. The sky clouded over, it began to get dark and all at once I realized that I might be in for some trouble. I broke out of a thick black growth to see the moose enter more of it three hundred yards across a small open bog, so I quit right there.

I backtracked and found high ground just before dark and didn't dare do any more traveling. There was plenty of dry cedar and other wood around the base of the ridge, so I built a fire against a slightly overhanging rock and began to drag up wood for the night. I wished fervently for an axe, but had none, and even though I gathered what I thought was quite a large pile of wood, it was gone long before morning.

I won't say I was comfortable, because I was certainly far from it. Neither was I very easy in my mind, for I was not sure of my location and knew I could make a mistake and take in a lot of country before I found a warm bed and some grub again. I can see no particular charm in squatting before a smoky fire all night wondering whether you are going to be lucky enough to get home the next day or the day after, and although I like a certain amount of privacy, I do not care to have it in such large doses all at once. I *thought* I was close to the east end of the ridge where the old camps were, but I wasn't *sure*.

The more I tried to convince myself, the less sure I became, and when finally it got light enough to travel, I worked back along the high ground to the west and failed to recognize a thing until I suddenly came upon the camps. From then on it was easy and I was eating beans and bread in the cook room at ten o'clock.

I sent downriver for a good stout belt, a heavy hunting knife, and a sheathed belt axe. I riveted the knife-sheath to the belt on the left side and the axe-sheath on the right, and from then on when I went out to get lost, the first thing I reached for was that belt.

Along toward the middle of October, I was on my way down from the camp above us on the river. I had been making a little social call, had had lunch with the timekeeper and started back to my own outfit a little late. There was a spotted trail between the two camps for a distance of four miles, running about half a mile back from and parallel with the river. It hadn't been used much and the tree-blazes were few and far between.

When I had covered about a mile of the distance I had to go, I looked down a hardwood slope to my right to see a very nice buck standing half-concealed by a small fir about eighty yards away. The cook had been kicking about the scarcity of fresh meat in camp (we were allowed a couple of deer in those days) so I swung the sights of the little .250 Savage onto the deer and let her go. He went out of there flapping his tail, and took off down toward the river. I shot only once, for I was quite sure he was hard hit, and the nearer the river he went, the better it was for me, since I could pick him up by canoe easier than by horse.

There was a good blood trail at first, but after a time the flow grew less. The deer went toward the river, doubled back, turned toward water again and then seemed to set off in a fairly straight line somewhere about halfway between my trail and the river. At least, that's what I *thought*. The sky was overcast, dark came early and the blood trail dwindled to a drop now and then. Remembering my failings, I decided to cut sharp to my left, hit the marked trail and go to camp.

I turned abruptly north, hitched up my belt and made time. The only trouble was that the deer had already crossed the trail while I was hot after it, and with my eyes on the ground I had failed to see any of the spotted trees. After half an hour of very fast travel, I began to realize that there was something wrong with my calculations and turned south, but it was too late. I hit into an old tote road grown in head-high with brush, pulled down it a way, lost it and then wound up in the worst tangle of a blow-down I ever saw. The trees, mostly hemlock, were bare of bark and dry, the bleached branches as dangerous as barbed wire.

It was nearly dark and, knocking off some dry limbs with my light axe, I made a quick fire in front of one of the fallen trees. A few minutes' work with the axe and I had slanted some light poles against the back side of the trunk, covered them thickly with fir and hemlock boughs and had me a good windbreak and shelter. I made a thick couch with more boughs and was ready to gather wood for the night. There were plenty of dry hemlock branches close by, hard to cut but good firewood, and within the light of the blazing fire, I found a smooth eight-inch white birch. So I spent a not too uncomfortable night and actually slept a part of it.

In fact, I slept beyond daybreak and, since the morning was dark and cloudy, I had to do some guessing. I followed the old road back for half a mile or so and hated to leave it. A man hates to leave any kind of road when he is adrift in the wilderness, but as reasoning power returned with action and the light of day, I was quite sure that I had seen this road on one of the old Hubbard maps—the old Moosehorn Tote Road running east and west from Russell Stream to Chesuncook Lake. I wasn't sure which way I was headed, but everything seemed to indicate that I was traveling west. In fact, I had a very strong feeling, which may have been that much discussed "sense of direction" or even plain instinct, that told me to turn to my left, leave the old road and move in as straight a line as possible.

Ridge Runner

Now that of course is the right way to travel—when it can be done. But the theory when put in practice can offer some stubborn obstacles. A certain kind of swamp can be practically impenetrable, a tangle of blow-downs as bad. Unknown or unmentioned brooks, streams and beaver ponds can throw a man 'way off his course, and that straight line becomes a wearying series of cut-backs and detours that double the distance.

I had quite a time, but finally broke out on a horseback about three in the afternoon, went down the far side of it where I found a small brook and drank my fill. I built a small fire, pulled the breast from a grouse that I had shot and sat down to toast it on a stick.

Just then a man I knew—one of the company foresters—came down through the open growth and stopped by the fire. He had been downriver for a few days and was just returning to camp.

He said nastily, "Well, well, having a little picnic, or just catching up on your Scout work?"

I tried to think fast, but I was just too tired. "Whyn't you take that into camp," he went on, "and fry it up there? Won't nobody take it away from you."

I said, "It's too far and I'm too hungry."

He looked hard at me and began to grin hatefully. "Ha," he snorted, "too far! I know what ails you. You been out tomcattin' all night again. Bet you don't know where you are right now. You're still lost."

I remarked loudly and haughtily—much too loudly—that I was *not* lost; and then suddenly the statement became the truth, for I looked straight down over my fire and saw a nice big blaze on a tree. Since he had come from my right traveling toward camp, my way was perfectly clear. I had come out on the trail I had left the day before and the little brook was right on the edge of our slash.

I singed the bird and ate it; and although my forester friend made quite a funny story about that part, he could never prove that I didn't know where I was when I built the fire.

I got lost many times after that in widely scattered localities. I would go out, perhaps on a Sunday, and when I didn't show up at dark somebody would say, "Where's the clerk? Bet he's gone and got lost." And the foreman, the blacksmith or the cook—somebody who knew me—would say, "Well, it's about time. He ain't been good and lost for more'n two weeks. He'll probably stay out three or four nights to make up for it."

You see the most beautiful and unusual things when you are traveling alone. There are people you would give the world to share them with, but such things are seldom shared. Two or more people pull against each other. Each may wish to take a different path, and the weaker or more amiable defers to the more insistent even though he knows his way is right. Two men make more noise and throw off more scent than one, and wild life in consequence is shy and moves away. While alone, even though I was lost some of the time, there was no one to urge me into different trails or complain when I took the wrong ones. I had only myself to consider, so things came out all right.

Once I came out of a dark valley, climbed a sharp ridge, went down the other side and suddenly came out onto the shore of a beautiful little lake with water as clear as crystal. It was rimmed with white sand and great towering boulders, and a mountain went straight up from the far side leaving its duplicate faithfully reflected in the glassy waters. I was never able to find out the name of the lake and I will probably never see it again. I followed its outlet down to a stream, the stream to the river and thus back to camp.

Late one afternoon in the fall I came upon a little open bog covered thickly with crimson pucker-bush. In the middle of it was a small pond, dark and glossy as molten tar, with a lone spruce growing by it. The spruce tree and the pond were black as the blackest ink against the crimson carpet, and standing at the edge of the pool was a snow-white doe. A man could live a thousand years and spend them all traveling around the world, but he would never again see a sight like that.

CHAPTER IX

It is generally conceded that the lumbermen of thirty or forty years ago were pretty hard on the deer and moose population, but just how much damage they did is still a matter of conjecture and personal opinion. I have heard some stories that, if true, prove that when the law arrived on the scene, it was just in time; but I have never actually seen any of those reported slaughters in the winter deer yards take place, although I have talked with men who claimed to have taken part in them. I do know that camp hunters were employed as late as my time, but they were not on the payrolls as such and many of them were not nearly as good as they thought they were. I was offered one such job in 1916, but the offer came from an outfit that I didn't like, so I turned it down for that and other reasons. I think most of the camps had fresh meat quite often; in fact, some of them had venison so often that the crews kicked. One of my superintendents became very indignant indeed when, during my first two weeks in camp, I put in a requisition to the depot camp for a side of fresh beef. "Why," he complained to the head clerk, "I never heard of such a thing. Here it is right in October, tons of fresh meat runnin' around that camp on the hoof, an' that lazy penpusher askin' for beef. Better get rid of him an' hire somebody that can do a little butcherin'."

I knew that there were certain laws governing the killing of deer and the taking of fish, but we also had a prohibition law. Nobody seemed any more enthusiastic about enforcing the game laws than the one on liquor. So why worry?

Road and dam construction crews were reported to be eating quite a few trout and salmon now and then, and sometimes they hit a small pond that yielded a killing. I heard of one pond near a road job that produced two sugar barrels of fine trout in one evening's fishing, but personally I never found any good trout fishing while on the early spring drives simply because I was too busy to move very far from where we were working; and while we were sluicing, if there were any trout or salmon in the stream, they just wouldn't bite. Later on in the season, after the logs had gone down, many of these brooks and streams proved to be excellent fishing waters, but by that time I was somewhere else. No doubt the frequent use of dynamite had something to do with conditions, but only once did I ever see explosives used in a deliberate attempt to kill fish, and the whole business from start to finish was ludicrous as well as nearly disastrous to the person most involved.

One of our driving wangans on Russell in 1916 was cursed with the most disagreeable, worthless, bigoted, puffed-up boiler of a cook that ever shoved a stick of wood in a cookstove. Now when you call a woods cook a "boiler" you are asking for trouble because you imply that all he knows is how to throw something into hot water. But this miserable travesty upon the name of cook couldn't even boil anything so that it was eatable

—he couldn't even turn out a batch of decent bread to sop up molasses. We had peas for soup, codfish (the kind that comes in one-hundred-and-twelve-pound bundles), a barrel of smoked shoulders now and then, and the regular flour, beans, pork and molasses. So with a little care and skill 'he might have fed us decently. He might have; but no, he was too busy posing around the camp, dressed up in one of those absurd white caps, imagining himself a "chef." Everybody in the outfit agreed that he "wasn't fit to lug guts to a bear," but the drive was short, we were stuck with him and my dislike for a certain species of Frenchman dates from the day I first met him.

Since one of the timekeeper's few small privileges is dropping into the cook room or tent and eating six or eight hearty lunches a day, this man's inability to produce sufficient nourishment of an appetizing nature antagonized me greatly; and when, after I had eaten some of his messes and taken his correct measure, he attempted to place the blame on me, as the supplier of bad and insufficient supplies, our relations became what is known as more than slightly strained. When at a later date he addressed me as *"garçon,"* my disgust turned to rage and loathing, and we entered into a state of total war. I don't know whether in his state of sublime ignorance he took me for a sort of steward employed expressly for his benefit or not, but when he called me *"garçon"* again and snapped his fingers at me, it was too much. I was able to establish only a small beach-head before the foreman pulled me off, but I made it known in no uncertain terms that the next time it happened the results would be serious. The boss was agreeable enough. He said, "All right, go ahead and kill the damned jilpoke and sluice him but remember you'll have to take over the cook room."

Well, that was the last thing I wanted to do, so I had to lay aside my ambitions and, as a result, this abomination of a grub-spoiler became more insufferable in his attitude than ever—that is until that great day, that memorable day, when he dynamited the trout in the rock pool in front of the wangan.

We let go a head of water from a splash-dam a quarter of a mile above camp and then shut the gates to build up another head. With the gates shut, the water in the stream was reduced to a mere trickle and along about noon I found a school of square-tails in a small basin scooped in a solid ledge at the foot of the roll-dam opposite our wangan. The basin was small, probably eight by ten feet, and I don't think there were more than a couple of feet of water in its deepest part. The trout—I could count seven nice ones—lay with their heads up under the logs of the roll-dam, and my mouth began to water when I thought of them browning in a big iron skillet of pork fat.

I hunted up a line, a hook, a few flies of various patterns, dug some grubs and went to work. I tried this and that and everything I could think of, but they were just not interested. I even tried gaffing them out with a bare hook and was busily engaged in this attempt when I heard steps on the bank and looked up to see that abhorred chef's cap with that imitation cook under it.

"Ho," he crowed vivaciously, "wat you do?"

I told him of a certain place he could go a long way from any running water, but he had already seen the fish and I knew there was no way to rid myself of him short of murder. Assuming an air of great importance and superiority, he gazed long at the trout, examined the pool very carefully, adjusted his cap to a more jaunty angle, and announced calmly that the acquiring of those fish was a matter of great simplicity. He would immediately take steps—he, Alphonse Légère, would demonstrate the taking of trouts as done under like conditions in his native land—that is, if I would at once procure for him the explosive of great power and in sufficient quantity.

I remained aloof and hostile until the significance of this word "quantity" burst upon me. Since a third of a stick of sixty percent stuff would have been more than enough to do the job, this demand for quantity served to acquaint me with the joyful fact that he knew less than nothing about what he was going to attempt.

I made a quick trip to the dynamite shack and came hurrying back with five sticks, a foot of fuse and a cap.

I asked him humbly and anxiously if he thought that the charge would be enough. He examined the pool again carefully, meditated, stroked his moustache, pulled at his ears and announced that it was indeed just barely possible—yes, with judicious placing the "bomb" might prove effective.

I then learned that the assembling of the "bomb" would be entrusted to my inexpert hands. Alphonse was not interested in construction, only in the actual sinking of the depth charge. So I punched a hole in one of the sticks, put a cap on the fuse, set the cap in the stick, soaped it well to waterproof it and then bound the whole five sticks firmly to an old cantdog hook which would act as a sinker.

I think he hoped at the last that I would perform the final act for him, but, pleading ignorance, I forced the charge into his reluctant hand and together we walked over to the edge of the pool and stood on the shelving bank about four feet above the water. He had to strike four matches before he could make the fuse catch and, finally, when it began to spit fire, he was in a decided hurry to get rid of it. He tossed it hurriedly into the shallow basin just below the roll-dam and, when I saw it hit the water, I moved and moved back fast for about seventy-five feet and then dropped flat. He started to follow me, stopped, looked back and then ran to the edge of the stream again.

I yelled, "You damned fool, come away from there. You want to get killed?"

He stepped back from the bank a little, placed his hands upon his knees, stooped and peered intently into the water and squalled, "You ain' feex heem good—she don' go!"

He straightened up, turned and took one step toward me—and she went!

Now, when a charge of dynamite goes off on the surface of a solid ledge scantily covered with water, the blast goes up and out with a most ungodly, ear-splitting crash. I was looking straight at him when the concussion hit him and I remember quite vividly that I saw him blown clean from under that high, white cap. The cap stayed where it was: he just went out from under it and left it there in the air. He hit the ground 'way ahead of it, but the shock did not kill or even cripple him. He was not in the best of health for quite a few days, but perhaps on the whole the experience did him good—spiritually if not physically. Anyway, from then on until he left us, he showed a very humble and contrite disposition as well as a tendency to duck wildly at any sudden noise. The boss had quite a lot to say to him about the affair, for the logs in the roll-dam were up-ended and had to be replaced; and while that job was being done, I discovered a smear of what, with some difficulty, I identified as part of a trout's belly plastered against a tree, so we can safely assume that the explosive was indeed of great power and in a little more than sufficient quantity.

Although I am not an inveterate fisherman and no expert in the art of presenting natural or artificial lures to reluctant trout, I think that over a period of years my family has eaten about as well if not better than the average. After about thirty-five years of fishing, cussing and trying various monstrosities in the form of hair, fur and feathers, all guaranteed to catch fish, I have reached the conclusion that when fish, especially brook trout, get ready to rise and feed, if you are on the spot with reasonable offerings there will be trout in the frying pan. However, there are days when, although the water may be full of trout, it is impossible to take them on the better known patterns of flies, but they will rise eagerly to some freak that resembles nothing that ever flew or crawled.

I spent a whole summer at Seboomook one year and had a chance to check on a lot of fishing theories. There was ample time for fishing, and I caught some very fine trout and salmon in the river below Seboomook Dam.

Ridge Runner

Russell Stream had not been driven for several years, and I had fine sport in those waters that had been barren of trout when I had last fished them. A small body of water called Lost Pond, up on the side of Russell Mountain, proved uncertain and tricky: although it was full of trout, it was impossible to predict whether they would rise or not. I fished it several times before I found trout fairly boiling in a shallow cove where some sort of food was concentrated. I took what I needed, hooking a trout at nearly every cast. By carefully watching the wind and weather, I managed to repeat this performance several times. These trout came to a brown hair-fly with a painted yellow head. I don't know what it was supposed to represent, but it bore no resemblance to anything I have ever seen.

Right at the peak of the season a man from another state appeared at Seboomook and, having seen one of my baskets of trout, gave me no peace until I agreed to take him to Lost Pond. On a day when the sky was overcast and the wind in the right quarter, we put a canoe into the water and he went to work.

My companion was one of the finest fly fishermen I have ever seen. He was a dry fly purist and had the equipment to prove it—tweezers, magnifying glass, fly oil, clippers, and every other expensive gadget known to the trade, along with a bewildering assortment of dry flies, tapered lines and leaders, the finest three-and-a-half-ounce rod that money could buy and an expensive reel to match it.

We got out onto the pond about three in the afternoon, fished an hour and never got a rise. At four o'clock the water was like glass, not a ripple on it, and hundreds of trout came to the surface and began to feed all around us. We could see the little dimples, like heavy raindrops hitting the surface, as the trout opened their mouths and sucked something in. In a few minutes the air was full of tiny black gnats hovering low over the water, and the trout began to roll and splash a little as they fed.

My fisherman caught a gnat, examined it under his magnifying glass, matched it with an artificial fly from his fly box, smiled contentedly and began to lay his offering out among the feeding trout. He was an artist—no less. The artificial mingled deceptively with the real, for every time I spotted a series of dimples I would put him in a position to lay a fly on the right spot. The man never lived who could lay a prettier cast, but he got no rise. Calmly at first and then somewhat feverishly, he cut, snipped, examined, oiled, changed to flies a shade different in size and coloring and placed them over the feeding fish only to have them ignore the offering, sometimes taking a natural a few inches from where his fly rested. He was not a swearing man but the red began to creep up from his neck into his face, and his cast and recovery began to be a trifle vicious as the trout slowed their feeding and began to go down.

Finally he reeled in his line, shrugged a sore shoulder and said, "Well, young man, what do we do now? I've done everything that instinct and some quite extensive experience has prompted me to do and I'm beat."

I remarked somewhat apologetically that our Maine trout were crazy anyway, but I had a theory if he cared to try it—the theory of opposite extremes. If the fish would not take an almost exact imitation of the natural,

Ridge Runner

sometimes they would go for a glaring example of something entirely different—so different as to be absurd.

I expected to be laughed at but, surprisingly enough, he made no comment whatever and, when I handed him an old battered-up four-foot leader with two loops for snelled flies, he opened a fly book and produced a Royal Coachman of impressive size and a nameless bundle of feathers of a bright tangerine color.

He held it up. "What do you call that?"

I said that I didn't know, but to tie it on as a dropper and give it a try.

I shoved the canoe toward a little cove where the trout were still rising while he stripped off line and made ready for a cast.

He said, "How will I handle this fish-trap, anyway?"

"Just heave her out," I returned, "and start it back with a wet fly motion."

After a couple of false casts, the old leader and the two flies hit the surface with a splash. He brought in some line, that tangerine monstrosity came up, skipped the surface for a second and then a ten-inch trout took it in clear to the gills. He made quite a commotion landing that trout on the light rod, but we took it in and in fourteen casts he took eleven trout from ten to twelve inches in length. The old leader loop let go with the twelfth fish and he lost the fly.

He sat there and looked at the trout in the bottom of the canoe. His eyes lifted slowly to take in the mountains surrounding the little pond.

"Let's go to camp," he said. "Anything after this would be an anticlimax."

Ridge Runner

There are many people who profess to know all about fish and their habits. A man doesn't have to learn the hard way. He can sit by the fire and read just how it ought to be done; and then, equipped with the recommended gear, sally forth and do the job in a scientific manner. If the fish cooperate, feed by the book and agree that the various lures are worthy of notice, all goes well, but there are days when fish, especially brook trout, refuse to do anything according to rule.

It is a generally accepted fact that fish take their nourishment early in the morning or in the late afternoon and evening, but there are times when trout will begin to feed at the most unexpected and improbable moment. I remember one broiling hot day along toward the last of June up on the headwaters of Olamon Stream when trout started taking a wet fly worked ten or twelve inches under water. This was right in an open meadow with a bright sun beating straight down at twelve o'clock noon. The poorest kind of a day and right at the time when fish seldom feed—according to the book. Nobody but a fool or a person entirely ignorant of trout habits would have been fishing at noon on such a bright, hot day, but I took fourteen fine trout on a bedraggled Mickey Finn in as many minutes.

My grandfather used to say that the only time to go fishing was when "the sign was in their bellies," and thus far I have found no reason to doubt this statement.

It has long been conceded that one can travel the length and breadth of Maine, spread one's blankets in the deepest woods and encounter no animal that will offer physical harm. True, some wandering skunk or overfamiliar porcupine may cause some small inconvenience, but despite the tales of rampaging bears, the terrible Injun Devil and various strange crosses between wolves, bears and panthers that chill the blood and raise the back hair on a dark winter's night, there is little danger to the night traveler except that caused by his own carelessness.

Being a youth cursed with a vivid imagination as well as a wandering foot, I will confess that, while traveling through the gloomy depths of dense timber in that eerie twilight just before dark, I was prone to glance over my shoulder now and then, and no matter how many ways there may be of being scared I have experienced them all. There is a difference in being scared and being overcome by fear. Fright will freeze a person so that action is impossible, but when a man is merely scared, he goes somewhere or does something—fast.

When I went up across Moosehead for the first time, bears were an unknown quantity to me. I knew something about deer and other game animals, but my information on bruin had been sketchily acquired from reading somewhat lurid tales in various books and magazines supplemented by yarns told by the local hunters. I had a wholesome respect for the bear family in general although I was anxious to see one over the sights of my rifle.

There were plenty of bear around Pittston Farm—or so I was told. There were also hogs—several dozens of them—running wild in the near vicinity of the cleared land. They rooted around on the oak and beech ridges until cold weather brought them in for fattening and slaughter, and once in a while a bear got one. In fact, during the first week of my short stay there, the talk ran mostly to bears, and I was greatly interested in the conversation, so much so that shooting a bear became one of the most desirable things in life.

I had a big storehouse to look after, as well as a formidable amount of paper work, and the only time I could hunt was in the late afternoon. I would work until half-past three or four o'clock and then go hunting. I didn't have much daylight left to me, so I tried to cover as much ground as possible and get back near the road before dark. One evening after a week or so of this kind of hunting I stayed out too long, got into strange country, ran into a big beaver flowage where no water was supposed to be, and for this and other reasons became thoroughly confused. The sun was well down before I got out of the swamp, caught the last glow of sunset through the trees, oriented myself and, shortly after I had made sure of my direction, broke into an old logging road which I could follow. It wasn't much of a road, being full of old logs and downed trees, but it was better than taking to the brush and I was glad to follow it, since I was reasonably sure that it would take me out onto the gravel road near the farm. The faint glow in the western sky faded, and a few stars came out. The surface of the old road was thickly covered with moss and spongy mold, and the only noise I made was when I climbed over a down tree and broke a brittle branch.

It was altogether too quiet and a hell of a place in which to come on a bear. Various fire-blackened stumps dimly seen through the increasing darkness began to take up more and more of my attention. Off to my left, less than a hundred yards away, a buck blew shrilly, jumped hard into a brush pile and pounded away over the ridge. I went up and out from under my hat, and then stood for a moment to ease my breathing and wipe the sweat out of my eyes. The road became quite smooth and free from obstructions for a couple of hundred yards and I made good time. I felt that I was nearing the main road, which I was, and then there was this big uprooted tree down across the road about four feet off the ground, at its lowest point, near the tangle of roots and earth. I walked up to the trunk, shifted my rifle to my left hand, placed my right upon the tree and foolishly vaulted over it. I say foolishly because when my feet hit the other side, with all my weight and the impetus of my spring upon them, they came down on something huge, black and horrifyingly alive and vocal. I don't know whether I howled or not; and if I did, any sound that I might have made would have been drowned out by the ear-splitting roar that tore out of that creature's throat and went wailing off through the still autumn night. My feet went out from under me, my rump came down hard on struggling, heaving flesh, and then I was up and away. The animal went crashing off into the woods at my right while I bored a hole through the darkness, straight down the road. Luckily there were no more down trees in my way or I would certainly have been wrecked, but as it turned out I was only a short distance from the surfaced road, and very glad I was to get my feet on it and see the lights of the office only a short distance away.

Ridge Runner 161

The farm boss and the head clerk were standing in the open office door when I came into the yard. "You hear that hog squallin' over by the Beaver Pond Road?" asked the boss.

I said yes, and that probably they could hear him over in Canada. "Well," he mourned, " 'nother one gone. I wish to God you would kill that bear."

I went back at daybreak the next morning just to be sure. There were hog tracks all over the place—and one big hog skulking in the brush. I didn't get a very good look at it, because for some reason or other it was pretty wild.

There are automobile roads into that country now, but back in 1917 the only way you could get into the Sourdnahunk region was by way of the railroad to Millinocket and then over the Great Northern Tote Road up to Grant Brook, Abol and through to Foster's Storehouse and Number Seven. Beyond the camps at Abol the road climbed a gradual ridge until at its crest you could see before you the panorama of Katahdin in all its strange, grim, snow-capped beauty. The old road skirted the foot of the mountain and went on up by Sourdnahunk to the lake and, after leaving the south slope of Abol Pitch in the spring, it was like entering a different climate. The snow and ice may have been gone many weeks in Bangor and as far north as Millinocket, but even in late May one had to use snowshoes in those dark, secluded timbered runs and slopes north of Katahdin in back of the Brothers.

We had a camp and a new dam up on the headwaters of Little Sourdnahunk Stream, but when I arrived there early in May there was little sign of spring. The piles of pulp formed a solid frozen mass of spruce, covering the area where the pond would later be, but save for a light flow of water from the springs there wasn't much more than enough for camp use trickling down the stream bed.

For a month there was very little to keep me busy. I helped the head clerk at the depot, did some exploring and hunted bear. Nobody in the crews had ever killed any bear, but they all seemed to agree that it was a great bear country and, if one kept away from the deeper snow and hunted around the sides of the sunny slopes, there was an excellent chance of hanging up a bear skin. Just why my informants were so positive in their statements is hard to say for there are hundreds of good woodsmen who have spent all their lives in good bear country and never laid eyes on one. A bear seems to have little natural curiosity and ordinarily, at the slightest sign or scent of the unusual, he high-tails it into the brush and out of the way. A deer will stand and take that last look or depend on its natural camouflage for protection, but not the bear. He leaves at once and in a hurry.

I hunted the region quite thoroughly and found enough bear sign to assure me that they were coming out of winter quarters. I hunted until I got tired of packing my old 33 Winchester around and shifted to a belt gun. Convinced at last that I never would see a bear, I even neglected to strap on the pistol belt, and as the weather warmed and the snow began to melt, I had other things to think of.

To get to my outfit from the depot camp I had to go

north, cross Little Sourdnahunk where it emptied into the larger stream, take a trail up along the stream bed for a mile or so and then climb a steep bank to reach a burned-over plateau that stretched away for half a mile or more north of the stream. This open area was perfectly flat and devoid of vegetation except for a few blackened stumps and a sprinkling of young birch and poplar withes that would eventually fill in and cover the burn.

I had slept the night at the depot and came up the brook this bright, spring morning with no thought of bear in my mind. The sky was clear, the sun was warm, and the sound of rushing water bore witness to the fact that the snow was melting and we would soon have a head of water in the dam. The banks on the north side of the stream were bare and warm, and the steep trail up the side to the burn was soft with the melted frost in the gravel. I dug in my toes and went up the side of the eighty-foot slope with a rush, and then, as I neared the rim of the plateau, I slowed, crept noiselessly forward the last few feet, rested my hands on the ground and cautiously raised my head above the edge. I had no particular reason for this action, except that I had formed the habit when approaching open ground where there might be game. I had found out long ago that the less one was exposed the more there was to be seen, especially if the wind was favorable. Well, I poked my nose over the rim and looked the damndest, biggest, blackest bear in the whole State of Maine right in the eye. He was sitting on his haunches about fifty feet from me busily engaged in browsing on a bundle of birch sprouts that he had clasped to his bosom. He dropped the spring tonic and sat there with his paws drooped in front of him for a second or two and then—I don't know whether he took my old felt hat for a woodchuck or something else edible—instead of running, he dropped on all fours, kind of humped his back and took a step toward me. My heart gave a leap, slid over into my windpipe and then crawled up and filled my throat. It was incredible, impossible—nobody had ever heard of such a thing, but it was happening, and to *me!*

A phrase that I had heard flashed through my mind: "When they first come out in the spring, they are mean and ugly and will sometimes tackle a man." The bear took another slow, creeping step, and the tension that held me broke. I stood straight up, snatched off my hat, let out a wild howl and scaled the hat at him. He moved so quickly that he was just a dark blur of motion. There was a scuffling sound in the wet leaves and then he was off. I have seen some fast-moving objects but never anything that approached the urgency of this animal's get-away and the sustained speed of its departure. It seemed to bounce and roll out across the open burn like a big, black football propelled by some giant's boot, and the further it went the more that bobbing rump looked like an erratically bouncing black ball. I laughed until the tears ran down my cheeks while that bobbing, dipping, soaring ball grew smaller and smaller, finally disappearing into the small growth surrounding the burn.

A few days later I shot a bear over by the bog around Stink Pond. It may have been the same one, but if it was it had shrunk a lot in size.

Ridge Runner

We took our wood out of Little Sourdnahunk, drove it down the big stream and out into the West Branch of the Penobscot. In a few short days we were out of the cold, dank mountain valley and down where the new green of the poplars covered the burns and the air was sweet and heavy with the scent of arbutus. Our wangans came together to form one large outfit, and it was time for me to go.

We had been busy and secluded back in the mountain draws, but up the great rivers and over the lakes, through the high mountains and over the gentle timbered slopes the word had gone forth, and the young and rugged were dropping their axes and cantdogs, shouldering their war-bags and taking the trail toward the greatest adventure of all. I had wanted to leave much earlier in the spring, but there was no trained replacement for me and I felt strongly obligated to stick with the crew until things reached a point where one man could handle the work alone.

And so, at the break of dawn on a soft June morning, I shouldered my pack, picked up my rifle, said a few brief goodbyes and steered a course for Millinocket and the railroad.

The boss had said, "You don't want to go back up Sourdnahunk to hit the tote road. Go down the main river till you hit Katahdin Brook, cross over and pick up a spotted trail going northeast and along about nine o'clock you should hit high ground and Abol Farm. Take the road from there and it will save you a lot of time and walking."

It sounded fine, as do all such simple directions, but he neglected to mention half a dozen wide, deep logans reaching back inland from the river in some instances as much as half a mile, and neither did he mention the fact that before I hit the high ground at Abol, I would come out on the shore of Abol Pond.

I must have walked six or eight extra miles making my way around stretches of bog water, and when I had finally come to Katahdin Brook, made a crossing and then a little later found myself confronted with a very wet and sizable lake, I felt very low indeed. It looked as if upon this day of all days I had managed to get myself lost again.

The water in the pond was high and covered the trail around the north shore, but after taking a compass-bearing and traveling northeast away from the lake, I found high ground and hardwood and knew I was moving in the right direction. The ridge grew more pronounced with gullies slashing it from left to right, but although the ground was wet and soft, there was no underbrush and I made good time. The air was warm and fragrant with spring, and when that first gagging whiff of putrid corruption filled my nostrils, it was like a slap in the face. It came eddying down wind from my left and I turned and walked down wind into a little run, quartering into the breeze. Low down, I lost the scent, but, climbing quietly up the opposite side of the depression, when I had nearly reached the top, it was stronger and fouler than before. I stood head and shoulders above the top of the bank and looked across to the side of the second run. There was a dead sow there—a grey-green putrescent mass of decomposed flesh and viscera into which an enormous bear had thrust its head clean to its ears. It was feeding voraciously, filling its lean hulk with that crawling, stinking mess; slobbering and gobbling like a hog in a tub of swill. It pulled its head out of the burst belly and turned it toward me, the face even above the eyes covered with greenish slime. It couldn't have seen me because it turned toward the carcass again and I shot it back of the left ear.

I know a lot of people profess to like bear meat and I have eaten it myself when there was nothing better offered. A young bear fattened on beechnuts is supposed to be something pretty nice, but I must confess that my stomach still squirms when I think of that scene back of Abol Farm, and I will trade the finest roast of bear for a can of corned beef any time.

I left the bear, went straight up the ridge and in less than ten minutes came out into the road just above the buildings at Abol. I was wet to the waist, tired and hungry, but after I had put away a loaf of fresh "riz bread," a quart of beans and half a dried apple pie, I felt better. "If you want a bear skin," I told the cook, "you'll find one a quarter of a mile down back of the buildings on top of an old dead sow. The hide is still stuck to the bear and it's pretty well rubbed, but it's a big one."

"Heard the shot," said the cook. "Figured you must have run onto sunthin'. That there bear has raised merry hell around here, killed our shoats an' broke into the storehouse. Made a mess of things. Like to nail that hide on the barn door an' soon's I get cleaned up some of us will go down an' rip it off." He grinned and stroked his handlebar moustache: "Didn't fling no hat at this one, did ye?"

After I had rested a while, I went on to Grant Brook, laid up there over night and made Millinocket early next morning.

Of all the places I had ever been the Sourdnahunk Valley was the most fascinating and the most beautiful. I left it with regret, promising myself that some other spring I would return again for another bear hunt, but I never did. Things just don't seem to break right at times, and the years go by very swiftly after you get to a certain age. I no longer have that burning desire to shoot bear and, even if I did, I doubt if luck would ever favor me to the extent it did that spring back in 1917.

CHAPTER X

WHEN I was discharged from the Army in 1919, bearing no scars from the desperate battles of North and South Carolina, I found some difficulty in getting placed in a job similar to the one I had left, and it was not until the spring of 1921 that I succeeded in making the right contacts and went north again. They sent me up to Ten Mile on the Rockwood-Pittston Road, but how things had changed! The work was familiar, the pay adequate, but there was none of the old foot-loose freedom. Clumsy, snorting tractors and fleets of freight trucks had replaced the tote-teams except in the most remote places, and the volume of paper work had increased to an extent where a man had to stick close to his desk and telephone if his work was to be done efficiently. There was no opportunity for hunting, fishing or exploration and, although I handled the job well enough, I was restless. It seemed to me that if I had to be confined to an office I might as well suffer in civilization where I could have my wife and baby with me. So along in the middle of the summer I took a transfer to the accounting department of the Bangor office.

I wore a neat suit, a clean shirt and a stiff white collar to work every day and received a salary equal to that of the bookkeeper at the granite works at home. My mother was very pleased, but I coughed and began to hear my heart thumping. The flesh melted from my bones and after six years of office drudgery I had to make a change. In fact, during the next five-year period I made several changes, none of them very good or lasting, although I rode a pretty high horse just before the depression and, when I fell, I fell hard.

I took the game warden's examination in the fall of 1932 and received an appointment in October, 1933. I accepted this appointment because I wanted an outdoor job, and working for the State seemed to offer a certain measure of security for myself and my family. I had a fairly good position with a chance for advancement, but I had taken a bad beating in the business world along with thousands of other small fry and I felt insecure and a little afraid. Even though I had been away from the tall timber for some time, I had kept up my hunting and fishing, rifle and pistol shooting and, being sincerely interested in conservation, I felt that I could do justice to the job and entered this new field filled with unbounded enthusiasm.

The job of a game warden has always been a thankless one, but back in the days when I first went into the big woods the wardens were classed as a set of pariahs. There were some good ones, as the records will show—men who did their work without fear or favor and were held in respect even by the outlaw element. There were, however, enough political appointees with greedy ideas as to fees and travel to taint the name of the whole department, and many and bitter were the curses heaped upon the heads of these "sneaks" who reportedly backed down before determined opposition and grew fat on arrests made from the ranks of the poor and ignorant. No doubt most of these stories told in connection with wardens' activities are downright lies, but the ill reports together with the obvious desire of some officers to keep out of the woods and away from trouble caused many rumors to be stated as facts and the results were detrimental to the warden service as a whole.

I remember a story about one man in particular which left a bad taste in my mouth and caused the officer to be very unpopular. I met him several times in his official capacity and, although he seemed to be amiable enough, I could never summon up more than a mere pretense of civility toward him. As the story goes, this warden got caught in a bad blizzard somewhere up around Lower Grand Lake, and as a result of wandering around all day in the storm, he was in pretty bad shape when he blundered into a clearing where an old trapper had set up a base in a deserted lumber camp. The trapper warmed him, fed him and made him comfortable for two days, but made the mistake of feeding him almost exclusively on moose meat. The warden shoveled in the steak and biscuits while the storm lasted and then, when it cleared up, took a cut of meat and a piece of moose hide for evidence, and drove the trapper ahead of him out into civilization and into court. There was nothing the culprit could do but plead guilty, for there was a closed season on moose. With no money to pay a one-hundred-dollar fine, he spent sixty days in jail.

Now, of course, it might be argued that the trapper couldn't have been very bright to feed a stranger moose meat, but since that was all he had to offer and the warden ate well of it, it would seem that certain fundamental laws of hospitality had been violated, even though the officer was entirely within his rights. This story together with several others bearing on the activities of this particular warden did considerable to lower the prestige of the whole force.

One of the camp bosses told me of an incident concerning another warden who was supposed to be very tough.

"He showed up at my camp late in the afternoon," related the boss, "had supper with us an' looked the crew all over while he was eatin'. After supper he came into the office where the man he wanted was buyin' some stuff from the wangan. He asked this guy if he was so-an'-so, an' the guy said yes he was. An' this gun-totin' imitation of an officer says, 'Well, I'm takin' you down river with me in the mornin' to settle up for that little matter of four beaver pelts you run out an' sold last spring.'

"This feller he was tryin' to arrest was little but hard, an' he looks the warden in the eye an' says, 'You got the evidence?' An' the warden says, 'Yes, I got plenty.' Then this little feller says, 'Have you got a warrant?' An' the warden answers that he don't have no warrant and don't need none.

"'Well, mister,' says this criminal, soft and smooth, 'you go get you a good warrant, come back here with it an' I'll start out with you. I won't guarantee that we will both land where you're headin', but we'll make a start, mister, we'll make a start. But get this straight, mister—you ain't takin' me nowhere without a warrant, tomorrow mornin' or any other mornin', you understand?'

"Well, the warden pulls out of camp early the next day without his man an' I figured he'd be back in five or six days with his warrant. I had a talk with this alleged beaver poacher an' told him he better shoulder his turkey and hole up som'eres for a spell. 'Well,' he says, 'if you want me to leave camp, I will, but you don't think for a minute that bird will come back here with a warrant, do you? Hell, I know that big bag o' wind better'n I do you, an' I can tell you we've seen the last of him as far as this case is concerned.'"

The boss paused and spat contemptuously, "That feller stayed right in my camp all winter an' that yeller bastard of a game warden never did show up with a warrant. Now, what kind of a State officer do you call that?"

Now you take a goodly number of yarns like these, in which the wardens have been made plain damn fools, keep repeating and spreading them and, whether there is much truth in them or not, they are not going to do the individual or the organization any good. Their repetition fostered a contemptuous, antagonistic attitude among the woodsmen and guides that was very evident thirty years ago and still remains in certain sections of the State.

I believe it was around the middle of October, 1933, when I was sent down to Ellsworth to help Fred Smith, the warden in charge of that district. Whether or not I was of any help to him is a matter for debate, but I shall never forget the valuable assistance and patient instruction that I got from him. I received not only instruction, moral support and kindly understanding, but also material aid in the shape of food, shelter and even cash. I also got the damndest going-over in the shape of work and travel that a novice ever got during a training period, and I profited greatly thereby.

Warden Smith (now retired) was one of those thin, long-geared, slightly stooped woodsmen who move at a half-trot all the time, and since I had to take two steps to his one in order to keep up with him, I expended just twice the effort in going from here to there on foot. I had a brand-new pair of leather-top hunting rubbers that were hard on the ankles, and there were times when I thought my feet were being slowly skinned. Warden Smith was unmarried but kept a comfortable home just outside of Ellsworth. Just why, I don't know, for he evidently used it only as a place to take a bath once in a while or to store his gear. When I approached the point of total collapse and my feet got so sore that I began to fall behind and limp pitifully, he would relent and once or twice a week allow me to sit in a chair, bandage my skinned ankles and sleep in a bed with a mattress on it.

Most of the time we were on the move. He had a sleeping bag, a closed car and a portable gasoline stove. There was a grub box in the car, packed with supplies, and rain or shine we rammed over the back roads, checked camps, checked hunters, looked over spawning beds, watched for illegal trapping, and then when daylight ended, lay out near some secluded clover patch watching for jackers.*

---

* Jackers: Those who illegally jack deer at night by the use of spot (or jack) lights.

Ridge Runner

He cooked our meals on the gas stove and sometimes, when the weather was rough, inside the car. We washed and shaved each morning on the shore of some icy lake or stream and ate tremendous breakfasts of sausages, ham and eggs or cube steak; and then after washing the dishes and changing our socks, we were off again in search of trouble.

Snow came early that year and the nights were cold. I had a couple of old mill-felt blankets and a piece of tarp for a bed-roll, and used to envy Fred's hearty snores while I shivered and shook on the frosty ground. Usually I would get frozen out before full daybreak and by the time he woke up I would have the stove going and a little fire for heat. He would poke his bald head out of the sleeping bag, grope for his cap, pull it on, glance at the grey dawn and say, "Well, well, nothing like ambition in a young man. Must have overslept again. How'd *you* make it?"

I would groan out the sad fact that I had nearly frozen and hadn't slept a wink.

He would eye my thin bed and cluck dismally, "Too much beddin'. It smothers you an' shuts off circulation."

I will never forget the first day that I worked alone. Fred had some personal business in Ellsworth to look after, so he drove to the outlet of a small pond and told me to go down the brook and look for traps. He said he knew the brook was being trapped by a certain man and he wanted me to be sure to find any unmarked traps or any other sign of illegal trapping. He impressed upon me that this particular trapper was a bad hombre and that it was just possible there might be a little trouble that would test my ability as an officer.

It was early in the morning when I began to move carefully down the little brook, watching every hole and narrow riffle for a set. The tracks of a man showed plainly here and there in the soft mold beside the brook as I progressed slowly and quietly. There was a big moss-covered boulder in my way and, creeping softly around it, I came upon a little pool bordered with yellow sand and smooth pebbles—a miniature lake set among the dark hemlocks in the twilight of the little valley. By the shore nearest me, in about three inches of water, sat a yearling raccoon. He crouched there looking at me with a weary, puzzled look in his eyes, and then I saw the trap clamped just above his right front paw. He sat up, slipped his left paw under the trap to take the weight of the trap off his injured leg, and held the steel out before him as if to say, "Look at this horrible thing that has happened to me. Do something about it."

My instructions had been positive, "If you find anything in a trap, leave it there and wait for someone to come and take it out." I could see the whole of the trap and the entire length of the chain from the trap to the toggle end where it was fastened to an exposed root. I looked and looked, but there was no sign of the metal tag that should have been attached, bearing the trapper's name and address. After a while I left the brook and went up the bank on the opposite side where I could watch the pool. The 'coon whimpered a little and settled down again with all four feet in the shallow water.

I could see up and down the brook for about fifty yards. Just above me the brook bed widened to form a little open swamp, and in about half an hour a big, sleek dog fox came into the opening about thirty yards from me. He peered around with his near-sighted eyes, investigated several grass tuffs, worked up the brook a short distance and then crossed. I slid my .45 Colt from its holster, cocked it and lined the sights on him, but just as I was about to press the trigger, I remembered what I was there for and that a shot would give me away. The fox wandered off up the brook, and I settled back to watch for my trapper.

It was close to noon when I heard a twig snap and saw an old man hobble around the bend and into the opening above me. He had on a tattered brown overcoat belted with a harness strap, the brim of his stained old hat dropped around his hairy ears and he shuffled along using a stout stick as a cane. The raccoon raised his head and wrinkled his nose in a snarl, and when the man crept around the boulder to the pool, the little animal showed its teeth and backed away to the full length of the chain. The trapper took two slow steps, struck once with the heavy stick and I slid down the bank, my heart pounding.

The man seemed greatly disturbed as I jumped the brook and confronted him. His hands shook so that he could hardly spring apart the jaws of the trap to remove his catch.

"Guilty, guilty as hell," I thought as I asked him for his license. I felt no joy at the prospect of taking this decrepit old hulk into court.

His license was in order and I said, "What about this unmarked trap? Is it yours?"

His poor old jaw began to shake. He looked at the

trap, fumbled with the chain and then quavered, "Before God, mister, that trap had a marker on it when I set it. It was down on the toggle end of the chain an' this here 'coon thrashin' around must have tore it off. Clost to fifty year, I been trappin', mister, an' never been in trouble. You ast Fred Smith about me—he'll tell you."

I said reasonably, "Well, if there was a marker on the chain, it must be right here around this pool somewhere, so let's find it."

So we began to scan the shore of the pool carefully and in a very few minutes I found the brass tag partly concealed in a tuft of moss.

Talking it over afterward with Fred, I asked, "Why, if the man was in the clear and knew it, did he show so much sign of fear?"

"Well," said Fred, "put yourself in his position—quietly going along about your business only to be suddenly confronted with a wild-eyed individual with a hog-leg a foot and a half long slung to a cartridge belt with four pounds of .45 slugs in it. I'm supposed to be the only warden around here, and he probably thought you were one of the James boys come to life. What would you have done with the old cuss, if you hadn't found that trap-marker?"

I thought that over for a minute and then had an inspiration. "Well," I answered brightly, "since he was in your district, I would have turned him over to you, of course. And then, what would *you* have done?"

"Shot him," he answered sourly. "I would probably have shot him and let him lay. You just turn your back on a desperado like him and it's hard telling what would happen."

I don't know how old Fred was when I traveled with him, but he must have been some over fifty, probably nearer sixty. He knew the country and the people for miles around and had an inexhaustible fund of anecdotes and stories dealing with places and individuals in his district. He had a quick, jerky way of getting his words out, and when he told a good story it was irresistibly funny. He would be riding by a certain farm or dwelling and he would begin to chuckle, "You see that old coot in the yard back there, well—" And then he would repeat some comical absurdity that would fix that person and place in my mind forever.

He had a story concerning an old man who lived on a farm just outside of Ellsworth. This individual, who was a rather excitable type, had a grown-up son who worked in one of the Ellsworth stores and was something of a sportsman. He liked to hunt grouse and woodcock, and once, when he was offered a promising setter pup at a reasonable price, he bought it and brought it home. Now to this boy's father a dog was a dog, something to have around the place to kill woodchucks and bark at strangers. Breed meant nothing to him, and anything over a dollar and a half for a pup was simply beyond his comprehension. The pup grew as all pups do, and one day, when he had developed into quite a promising bird dog and was pointing a meadow lark in the field opposite the house, a drummer drove by and stopped to watch him. The traveling man sat there in his rig for quite a few minutes and then accosted the old gentleman, who was sitting on the front porch:

"That dog belong to you, mister?"

The old gentleman said, "Why, what you want to know fer?"

"Well," returned the drummer, "I don't know but what I might like to buy him."

"H'm," said the farmer, "want to buy him, do you? How much you figger to pay?"

"Call him in," said the drummer, "so I can look him over and then I'll make you an offer."

So, the dog was called in, and the drummer examined him. "I really can't afford it," he said, "but I like the looks of this pup and I'll give you twenty-five dollars for him."

The old man's jaw dropped. He sat half stunned for a moment and then he let out a bawl, "Lucretia, bring out a plate of doughnuts and a pitcher of cider for this gentleman. Now, mister," he went on hurriedly, "that dog belongs to my son. If you will let me borrow your rig for a few minutes I'll drive in to town and talk with him. I jest *know* he'll sell at that price, so stay right here and rest yourself and I'll be right back."

The drummer agreed to the loan of his horse and buggy, and the farmer took off for Ellsworth in a cloud of dust.

The boy was busy waiting on customers and it was some time before his father could catch his eye. The old man paced up and down the length of the store until finally, trade slackened enough so that the boy had a moment free.

"Something the matter, Father?" he asked.

"Simmy," said the old man in a hoarse, agitated whisper, "Simmy, there's a dad-blamed fool of a drummer out at the house that is offering twenty-five dollars for that speckled hound of your'n."

"Hell," said the boy, scornfully, "I wouldn't take fifty for him."

The father stepped back as though from a heavy blow. He hasped, closed his eyes and wrung his clasped hands in a supreme effort to control himself, and then as the full enormity of this statement sank home, he cast his hat violently before him on the floor and raised his eyes and trembling hands toward the heavens. "Is it possible, O Lord," he raved in a choking bellow, "is it possible that Lucretia and I have labored all these years to bring up a goddamned fool?"

As far as results went, I proved to be a Jonah for Warden Smith. We worked and worked and combed the country far and near, but as I recall it, we made no arrests. I learned something of correct procedure and that an officer can be liked and respected throughout his district even though he may have a reputation for being rather strict. When I left Ellsworth and Fred Smith, it was with sincere regrets.

They sent me North around the first of November to take over a district up in the Enfield section. My north line was just south of Lincoln, the south line somewhere down in Township 32; the west boundary was the Penobscot River and God knows where the east line lay. We went through the usual fall routine, checking hunters days and hunting jackers nights with no glory or profit whatever to me. I had the mistaken idea that as long as a culprit was brought to justice, it made no difference who signed the warrant for his arrest, and my record of prosecutions remained very, very blank.

That winter was the worst any of the oldtimers could remember for a long time. It snowed and snowed and when it wasn't snowing the thermometer dropped to an unbelievable low. I had to live in my district, and since I could find no quarters for my family and couldn't afford to board, I had to find some kind of shelter and stick it out alone.

I holed up in a fishing camp at the outlet of Coldstream Pond near the fish hatchery. The building probably was comfortable enough in the late spring and summer, but a good dry bear's den would have been much more comfortable and easier to heat during such a winter as came down upon us. I had to haul my firewood in from the highway on a hand sled, and morning after morning I woke up to find an inch or more of dry snow on my bed. The water pail had four or five inches of ice in it nearly every morning. All my food froze solid, canned goods couldn't be used and eggs were like stones. Three feet away from the stove it was so cold that a man couldn't eat, and most of my meals were bolted straight out of the frying pan. The only way I could keep warm in the evening after supper was to go to bed and I didn't sweat any then.

The drifts and the banks thrown up by the plows went higher and higher until the roads were like white tunnels, and starting and driving a car was an adventure in itself. I had an open Ford Phaeton, a sheepskin coat and a pair of leather mittens lined with lamb's wool, and drove all winter without a sign of a cold. Days when it was not snowing too hard and the temperature was such that one could move around without danger of frostbite, I cruised the country on snowshoes. I went

up the Passadumkeag River to Lowell and the surrounding swamps, checking for deer yards and on game conditions. I found the largest series of yards I ever saw or heard of up in the Rollins Ridge section and walked for miles in the deer paths through the cedar swamps without snowshoes. There were dozens of cast antlers around some of the open springs, but I was never able to pick up a good matched pair. All the deer from the east side of Coldstream Pond and those in the towns of Enfield and Lowell must have gone into those yards, because one could travel for miles on the ridges east of them and never see a deer track.

Down at the head of Nicatous Lake and around Big and Little Sabeo, Horse Shoe and Green lakes the deer were in bad shape. It was impossible for me to get in there under the conditions prevailing, but, as soon as the lakes were open, I made the trip by canoe and found that all around the shores the deer had eaten every vestige of vegetation as high up as they could reach. Down on Brown Brook in the district below mine a bunch of deer yarded on the ice and bid fair to starve to death, with several acres of young cedar not over three hundred feet from them. We got permission from the landowners to cut cedar for them while the snow was deep, for they stubbornly refused to use the trail we broke for them into the midst of plenty.

One day around the first of February the wind shifted into the south some time during the night, and it rained for two days. Water poured out of the dark, low-hanging clouds as though it would never stop. The high-banked roads became small rivers of running water. During the night following the second day, the wind died and then came strongly out of the northwest, while the mercury dropped to thirty below. The roads were now solid ice, and there was a crust in the open that would almost hold a horse. The clear, cold weather held for a week, and I cruised out a lot more country that I previously hadn't seen. Without snowshoes one seemed strangely light and free, and I covered much ground but found nothing new except that the deer had left their yards and were traveling everywhere over the crust.

They scattered far and wide, enjoying the feel of something solid under their hooves and the sense of unlimited space to move in. And then it snowed. The blizzards came howling down out of the northeast and the terrible storms caught them bunched under overhanging banks, narrow stream beds and deep gullies where there was no winter feed, and they died miserably by hundreds of starvation and exposure.

The winter of 1933-34 was a long, hard drag, but outside of a few frostbites I managed to come through in fair shape. The only trouble was that I couldn't seem to find anyone to arrest. I helped out on several cases, but prosecuted none of my own, and that was bad, very bad. The southern supervisor wrote me a nasty letter about not moving my family into my district (they would no doubt have been very comfortable in that fish camp), and when the snow finally melted and the spring floods came, when the Mayflowers bloomed and the trout began to rise, instead of feeling the joyful surge of spring within me, I felt low in spirit and filled with a vague unease.

That summer I combed the district day and night

and had no more home than a wolf. I bought a cheap sleeping bag, fixed up a grub box in my car and slept and ate, bathed and shaved wherever the need overtook me. The country was swarming with mosquitoes owing to the pools of stagnant water left by the extremely high spring flood, and during fly-time sleeping out every night proved to be quite an ordeal. The guides and most of the people seemed to like me. They said the country was quiet nights for the first time in years, and it looked as if I was really accomplishing something.

I bought a practically new tight board camp in Enfield village, put in a nice four-hole cookstove, sink, desk, a beautiful pine table made locally from two wide boards of native wood, and rigged up bunks for four men, with good mattresses, pillows and everything I could think of for comfort. By working on this project all summer on extremely bad days or early in the evening before I went out on night patrol, I finally had a warm, snug, complete base around the last of September. The chief came up, looked the district over and remarked that it was in the best shape he had ever seen it. I began to feel like a human again and then one day I went over to the post office after my mail and found a transfer down into the Rockland district.

I was lucky enough to sell the camp and all the equipment at no loss whatever to myself, and for that I was truly thankful. The chief down in my next division was a fine chap—sharp, intelligent and blessed with a strong sense of humor. He was quite frank in voicing his disappointment when I arrived on the scene, for he wanted a younger, greener man whom he could break in strictly according to his own ideas. We got along after a fashion, but when I finally got around to making some arrests, of course I had to go and pinch the wrong people. I made two bad mistakes of that kind and almost made a third. I lost a good moose case in superior court through inexperience, being obliged to conduct the case myself with no advice from anyone except the County Attorney.

I will say that my chief's jovial good nature was in evidence at all times. He even liked practical jokes and finally, when opportunity offered, he gave me both barrels. I have laughed to myself about it since, but the reaction was somewhat delayed. Several hundred other people have seen the funny side of the affair, too, for I have overheard sly remarks now and then—remarks made just loud enough so that I might hear and perchance react to the detriment of my dignity and to the joy of the listeners.

It began with a dead moose. Now dead moose are no novelty down in Knox County, for the animals are plentiful and the local gentry have no use for them. It would have been much more pleasant for me if the moose had all stayed up north where there was plenty of room, but for some reason or other they chose to take over Waldo, Lincoln and Knox Counties in considerable strength.

This particular moose had been dead some time when its demise was finally reported to me; in fact, even anyone with hay fever or bad sinuses could have smelled it at least two hundred yards down wind. I notified the chief and we drove our cars in to within a couple of hundred yards of the carcass and had no trouble at all in going right to it. It was a big bull with a pretty fair head and there was no questioning the fact that he had been dead for quite a few days. The rain had soaked the carcass, the warm sun had beat down on it and the body was swelled tight as a drum with gas. I believe even a hungry bear with a strong stomach would have given it a wide berth.

The chief looked the remains over carefully, walked around it a couple of times and said, "That is really a very fine head." I replied that it was a good head all right, but that the hair was slipping and it couldn't be mounted.

"Well," he returned, "I don't know about that. I think you better take off that head and cape. They will want it over in Augusta." I couldn't think what in hell they would want with that piece of carrion in the office at Augusta and told him so, but in return I received a positive order to take off the head and cape and deliver it to his residence. Then he went off about some urgent business and left me to do the job alone.

Now, anyone who has skinned out a head for mounting knows you have to make the circular cuts well down on the shoulders, split it up the neck where the hide is half an inch or more thick, peel the whole works up over the antlers and then find a certain spot just back of the skull where the knife will go through the spinal column and down through the whole neck. It is quite an operation even when the carcass is in the right skinning condition, and when the hair is slipping and the condition very far from right, it's no fit job for a man with a weak stomach.

The sun got hot, swarms of late fall bluebottle flies

arrived to plague me while I slashed and tugged at the stinking, slippery hide and finally got the cape off and the hide up around the head. Then I fought my way blindly to a dry knoll, cast myself down on my belly and retched until I thought my head would burst.

The head was off, but the job was only half done—I had to rope the mess together in some kind of carrying shape, rig a sling to get my arms into, horse the cussed thing onto my shoulders and then pack it two hundred yards out to the car. I had it out and tied onto the front bumper of the car about noon, and then I headed for Thomaston.

At the first running water, I stopped, stripped to the waist and scrubbed myself with a cake of yellow soap I kept in the car. I soaped and rinsed but I could still smell moose on my hands when I finally gave up and drove on into town. There were several customers in the small lunch room that I patronized, but shortly after I sat down at the counter, they began to fidget and squirm and then hurriedly called for their checks and left. Through the front windows I could see curious people making for the head on my parked car. They would advance with a highly interested air to within about fifty feet of it, whirl suddenly, grab their noses and cross over to the other side of the street. My sandwich and coffee came, but it was no use. When I lifted a hand within three inches of my nose, my stomach heaved and refused duty.

I paid and left, and the proprietor of the lunch room quickly began to throw open all his doors and windows.

The chief's wife protested bitterly at my leaving that head in her garage, but I explained that it was there by direct orders, dumped it in a corner and went away. Whatever became of it, I still don't know, but I *do* know that most of the clothes I had on were practically ruined and it was weeks before I could get the reek of rotten moose out of my nostrils. It was several more weeks before I could appreciate the humor of the affair and laugh heartily at the joke.

Along about the first of March I was transferred again, a good long distance this time, from Thomaston down the line to North Berwick, near the New Hampshire border. I paused briefly there among the scrub oak and scaly-barked pine, bounced over to the Songo River in Naples, stayed there through the smelting season, and then came gently to rest in Limerick over in York County.

I found a wise and understanding chief, good comrades all around me and plenty of poaching to keep me busy. They think down that way that I turned out to be a pretty fair warden. If I did, it was because the whole division took pains to show me the ropes, head me in the right direction and give me a memorable example of what loyalty and friendship can mean to a stranger in a strange land.

CHAPTER XI

It is a matter of record that, from the beginning of any organized form of government, the poaching of fish and game has been going on, and it will probably continue as long as there is any wildlife left to us. We natives of Maine are a stubborn, individualistic people who bitterly resent any intrusion on our rights, and the right to bear arms and use them is one of our jealously guarded constitutional privileges. It is unfortunate, however, that some of us refuse to identify ourselves with that mythical "State"—that vaguely defined institution which makes all the objectionable laws and insists on having them enforced. Every law passed by the State legislature, and in consequence enforced by properly appointed officers, is presumably the result of a decision by a majority for the good of the whole. But a lot of us, not entirely ignorant, insist on laying all the blame on "those crack-pots over in Augusta."

Unfortunately the laws relating to the taking of fish and game must be drawn up in such a manner as to provide adequate penalties for intentional and habitual offenders and leave as small a loophole for evasion or escape as possible. When an unintentional transgressor gets involved in these toils, I believe it is entirely up to the official handing out justice whether leniency shall be granted, and not up to the arresting officer. No one can offer as quick and smooth an explanation when caught in the act as the man who goes out deliberately to break the law. He has his plans made, his speech rehearsed and he knows just what is coming to him. If he is a stranger in the warden's district, he will rely on a frank and sad story of inexperience and gross ignorance, and sometimes he will get away with it.

I remember of one instance where two ragged and forlorn-looking culprits pleaded their extreme poverty and distress so well that they fooled both a trial justice and myself. One of them sat with his head drooped upon his chest, a picture of dejection, while the other, weeping openly, raised trembling hands pitifully and beseeched the judge, "We didn't know it warn't legal to fish in that lake. Somebody told us there was some good pickerel there an' that it was all right to fish. So we come up an' took these three fish an' the warden caught us. We ain't got a damn thing in the house to eat but half a loaf of bread, a little salt an' a small piece o' pork; an' I figgered these fish would give us a couple of good meals. We ain't never been in no trouble before, an' if we get fined, we'll jest have to lay it out in jail." He choked, sobbed heavily, and it was almost more than I could bear.

The judge took me into another room and whispered hoarsely, "What in tophet did you bring those two in here for? Why didn't you take the fish and let them go?"

I said, "You know I don't do business that way. *You* let them go if you want to, but I think they should pay the costs of court, even if you have to give them ten days or so to do it in."

"Well," he reflected, "they may be telling the truth and then again they may not. Anyway, we'll see what happens."

We went back into the room where court was held.

The judge said, "The minimum fine for this offense is ten dollars, but I am going to remit the fine upon the payment of the costs which amount to four dollars and eighty-five cents for each of you—nine dollars and seventy cents."

The "Weeper" sniffled glumly, and then whined, "What about them fish? Can't we keep them fish for our supper?" He had addressed himself to me and I told him I had turned the fish over to the court and that it was up to the judge, who was now writing busily on the two warrants.

The judge looked up and said, "You pay those costs of nine seventy and you can take the fish for all I care. We don't want to see you go hungry."

The lachrymose old scoundrel leaped spryly to his feet, dashed away his tears with a dirty hand, reached into a pocket and pulled out a wallet so fat with bills that it would hardly bend. He felt around amongst the currency, laid down ten dollars, scooped up the thirty cents in change that the judge somewhat dazedly placed upon the table, grabbed the three four-pound pickerel and the two of them slid through the door as spry as a couple of weasels.

The judge was old, experienced and supposed to be full of guile. We looked at each other in comical dismay for a moment. "Well," he offered somewhat feebly, "once or maybe twice in a lifetime I get really taken in."

A couple of days later I met the warden south of me.

He said, "I see by the paper you had two of my customers in court the other day."

"You mean those two old reprobates are regular customers of yours?"

"Hell, yes," he laughed, "those two will pull anything. I usually have them in before a judge at least twice a year."

When an officer gets caught like that just once, he becomes suspicious of especially vehement denials of guilt and, although there may be some few instances where he can use his judgment in setting aside or refusing to notice some small technical violation of the law, during the course of a year's work these cases are few and far between. All wardens are warned constantly that they are not to persecute the public and that the average citizen is not to be considered in the same class with the deliberate offender, but I have never in my years of active service learned to tell the sheep from the goats. We have serious fish and game law violations perpetrated by people in all walks of life—business and professional men, teachers and even the clergy—and it is surely unfair to judge a man by his clothes or the tone of his voice. Because a man wears torn overalls and broken-down shoes and fails to shave regularly, his appearance may be a little against him, but it is surprising what is sometimes found in the creel of the gentleman with fancy waders and a fifty-dollar rod. The offences being the same, I am inclined to favor the guy in the overalls. He is not supposed to know a whole lot, but the gentleman with the fancy rigging and the lodge ring should have brains enough to keep out of trouble.

I have an abiding faith in the fundamental honesty

of my fellow citizens except in those matters pertaining to our natural resources. The very fact that a bird or animal is in the wild state, unfenced, unbranded and classified as "game" seems to enliven that spark of cruelty and feed the primitive desire to kill that lies deep within most males and some females.

It is hard to explain the impulse that will cause an otherwise gentle and well-brought-up youth, with the best of school and church affiliations, to shoot a load of birdshot into a deer when he knows the act will cause only suffering and an eventual lingering death to a harmless animal. Or why a kind and indulgent father, driving his automobile along the highway on a family outing, will deliberately plunge his car into a huddled flock of young grouse, leaving a crushed and bloody mass of feathers behind him. But the desire to kill is there, and the length to which some people will go in order to escape the consequences of deliberate violations of the laws relating to the taking of fish and game are amazing and often ludicrous. A solemn oath means little, and perjury is an ordinary occurrence in courts handling these cases.

Evading the law about one deer per hunter proves especially popular during a season when the animals are plentiful. It is amazing to observe the number of Dianas the State of Maine can produce from among its womenfolk when deception is needed to cover up for a second deer in the larder. When you see a prospective mother obviously in the advanced stages of pregnancy, her body swollen to the point where it is an effort for her to stand up or sit down, raise her right hand and swear before God to tell the truth the whole truth and nothing but the truth and then go on the witness stand and testify that two days ago she not only shot a deer but struggled seventy-five yards through a thick growth of ground hemlock to cut its throat personally and put her tag on it, you've got to admit she is quite a gal, especially when her testimony remains unshaken owing to a certain leeway which the prosecution must allow for her delicate condition. This woman was a good witness for the defence—good enough so that the State lost the case and the officer making the complaint was bitterly censured in the public prints for requiring her to appear in court at all.

We had a couple of years when apparently it was the easiest thing imaginable for large numbers of housewives to go out and kill a deer. They just shed their aprons, dusted the flour off their hands, skipped down to the town clerk's office, got a license and sometimes within a half-hour would be at the inspection station with a deer to be tagged. Some of the stories told by these ladies were interesting, but in most cases failed to agree with their husbands' accounts of the hunt by a wide margin. Some of these Amazons were really quite clever, a very few actually killed their deer, but most of them, when courteously urged to offer an explanation concerning their unusual luck when hundreds of expert hunters were carefully combing the woods with little or no success, became most satisfactorily voluble and let their tongues run away with them:

"Oh yes, I tagged my deer yesterday morning about nine o'clock. Where did I shoot it? Up back of that old orchard as you come into the North Road by the old sawdust pile. How did I happen to go hunting that

Ridge Runner

morning? Well, I was washing the breakfast dishes, and Harold—that's my husband—came in and said there were some deer up by the old orchard by the sawdust pile and why didn't I shoot one, so I put on my coat and we drove down to the town clerk's and got my license.

"No, we didn't go right up there then. We went home and I got my .22 rifle. I shoot real well with a .22, cans and things, and then we went up by the orchard and there was a deer standing there. Oh, yes, I was awful excited. I had never shot a deer before. Where did I aim? Well, now, let me see. Oh yes, I aimed right at the neck. With the .22? Yes, with my own little .22. I aimed at its neck, pulled the trigger and it fell down dead. Oh yes, it bled a lot. There was a great big nasty hole in its neck and it bled and bled. (The great big nasty hole was where Harold had cut its throat long before she ever saw it.) It made me kind of sick.

"What kind of a rifle does my husband use? Well, it's a great big one that makes a terrible noise. There is a thing on it like my .22 that you pull back and forth. I think they call it a bolt gun. Yes, my husband is out with it now. You see, we have a lot of company around Thanksgiving and he wants to get another one before the sports get too thick and stir them up. We really need two deer, especially this year—look, here are some of his cartridges. (Half a box of 220 grain soft point 30-06 shells presented for inspection.)

"Where's the deer now? Well, it's all cut up, and all except one hind quarter is in cold storage in Biddeford. The hide? Well, that hide must be around the place somewhere. Yes, it's all right for you to go look for it. Go right ahead; we have nothing to conceal."

We find the head and hide of a nice doe rolled up and tucked into a corner of an old shed out back of the barn. It has a thirty calibre hole in the left side back of the shoulder and at the point of exit on the right there is an opening the size of a half-dollar. To make things perfect, just as we finish looking the hide over Harold drives into the yard with another deer—a fine buck. Poor Harold!

Once in a while a man will unwittingly inflict just punishment upon himself and suffer greatly thereby, even though the hand of the law hovers but does not fall. I remember the predicament in which a friend of mine found himself during a certain fishing trip. Slightly fuzzy from a generous helping of Hand Brand alcohol flavored with juniper extract, he found himself in possession of seven trout of doubtful length while the local game warden worked his way down the stream to check his license and look at his fish. My friend, showing very poor judgment in this critical moment, scooped up the trout and dropped them into the leg of his knee-length rubber boot. This happened about four p.m. on a very warm day.

The warden proved to be an acquaintance of mine and, naturally, since my friend and I were camped near by, I invited him to eat supper with us. He accepted the invitation and spent nearly four hours with us, while my friend, a fastidious man about his personal habits and appearance, was obliged to walk around with those seven trout speedily reduced to a slimy mush that soaked through his woolen sock and plastered his foot and ankle with an odorous paste. By the time supper was ready he was so overcome by nausea that he couldn't eat a mouthful, and by the time the warden had left us his nerves were crawling with strain and sheer exhaustion.

His groans of relief when he finally got to the stream and soaked his odoriferous foot and leg in the cool, running water were pitiful indeed, but I lay awake half the night hugging myself with joy and trying to stifle my laughter. The more I thought about it, the funnier it seemed, but my friend looked at it from an entirely different point of view. He was quite cast down in spirit, thoroughly chastened, and I truly believe that that was the first and last time he ever placed his integrity in danger—or trout in his boots.

The part of the affair that really hurt him and amused me was the fact that the trout were really all of legal length. Because of the juniper juice or plain carelessness in reading the regulations, he figured a seven-inch limit on a six-inch brook.

Many episodes connected with the warden service are amusing, but there are others that fail to provoke much mirth. When you see an otherwise honest, upright and ordinarily responsible citizen reduced to a state of groveling humility because of a cut-up deer hidden in his car, or a full basket of short trout, there is nothing funny about it. When I hear, "Just give me a break this time. If this gets in the papers, it will ruin me," I can see my brother heading for the woodshed with my father close behind, a two-foot length of spruce lath in his hand, and hear the wail, "I didn't mean to do it, I didn't mean to, and I'll never do it again."

October in Maine is the finest month of all the year. The insects have gone, the nights are crisp and cool for sleeping and the days are warm enough so that one can roam the bird covers lightly clothed. When the hardwood slopes become a riot of brilliance and the sun at midday is too warm for violent exertion, one can just sit, look off across the hills and enjoy the flaming patchwork of crimson, green and bright yellow that only God can paint upon the mountain slopes. There are warm, still days when a thin, blue mist hangs over the hills and all the land is hushed, all the homely sounds of living stifled while this last warm magic burst of fleeting loveliness glorifies a dreaming world.

It is then that the bird hunters come with their smart guns and their sleek, lean dogs. When the leaves have thinned a little on the hardwood and the melting frosts of the early mornings hold the scent of grouse and woodcock, the flat bark of the shotguns slam against the sides of the rocky hills, echoing and re-echoing until, when several guns are working, there is a steady beat of rolling gunfire.

During this time there is a leisurely, pleasurable, carefree atmosphere in the hunt. The shooter, whether he is working an expensive dog or trying to kick his birds out of the covers alone, takes time to breathe, walks slowly and enjoys the beauty of the autumn woods. Killing is a secondary matter, and although the drag of a day's limit in the game pockets of the shooting coat may feel good to tired shoulders, the hunter usually considers himself lucky to bag a brace of birds in a day's shoot and his deepest satisfaction lies in the quiet enjoyment of a day outdoors.

Later when the white frost covers the ground in the morning and the grouse find sunny spots to warm themselves and pick up a little gravel from the roads, down in the southern counties the road hunters will have their innings, riding the gravel roads after the sun is well up to catch the birds either in the road or perching on those inevitable stone walls that border the country highways in southern Maine. On a cold, frosty morning the birds seem sluggish and reluctant to fly, and this road hunting when done by an expert is a sure way of putting pa'tridge in the frying pan.

We hit the high point of a grouse cycle in 1936 in some of the southern counties and saw some phenomenal shooting. There was a shortage of natural food in the covers and the birds came out on the country roads to feed on a small seed about the size of number four shot. These seeds came from a pod grown by a roadside weed, and the grouse went for them in a big way. Driving with my wife over a back road in the town of Parsonfield one afternoon in late October, we counted forty-two birds within a mile and a half. Three of them scuttled into the weeds at the side of the road as I stopped the car at the crest of a steep pitch, and when I got out and loaded the light Ithaca twelve that I was shooting, two of them flushed close to my feet and went straight out ahead of me in a narrow V over the deep valley. At the flat, double smack of the smokeless powder both of them crumpled in a fluff of feathers and fell almost straight down. It was one of the few perfect doubles in my life on those fast-flying southern birds, and for once there was someone along to witness it.

We had plenty of grouse to eat that fall and the one following, and my son who was just at "the eatin' stage" could put away a pair of birds, a couple of baked potatoes and half a dozen hot biscuits with no trouble at all.

We cooked them all kinds of ways, but the best method of all, to my way of thinking, is to fry them. Ordinarily, for a decent meal, one should figure on a bird to a person. After they have hung for three or four days in a cool, dry place, to dress the grouse, lay it down, pluck a few feathers from the breast laying the skin bare. Break the skin and then push it down toward the wings and back, leaving the breast meat clean and exposed. Then take the bird in the left hand firmly, grasping the legs and tail. Place the thumb of the right hand under the rear of the breastbone at the membrane of the abdominal cavity, push with the right thumb hard, and pull with the left hand. If the bird is in the right position, the legs, back-skin, feathers, neck and head will strip off into the left hand, leaving the clean breast and the two wings in your right. It is a matter of seconds to trim out the two legs and then you have the edible parts of the grouse free and clean. Take a very sharp knife and carefully remove the breast meat from the frame, wash all the meat, remove all shot, dark spots and any small feathers that have been driven in by the shot. Dry the meat with a clean cloth or paper towels, roll in flour and brown slowly in a generous amount of fat from the best smoked bacon obtainable. When the meat is golden brown, remove it from the pan and place it in a warm, deep serving dish. Stir a smooth flour paste into the hot fat until you have a rich, smooth, brown gravy. Pour this over the meat, place half a bushel of fresh hot biscuits within easy reach, draw up a chair and go to work. The meat should be so tender as to require only the use of a fork and one should steadily employ the fork with the right hand while sopping biscuits in the gravy with the left.

When the open season on deer begins November first, in the southwest part of the State where I have been stationed, there is an ominous change in the atmosphere. Although the very best of the grouse hunting may come in the first part of November, nobody thinks of birds any more. Long before daylight on opening day the roads are filled with cars, all hurrying to some previously selected spot where deer have been seen coming into the fields or where there is a well-known crossing. There is a new, nervous tension in the air. The dark metal of rifles, gleaming rows of cartridges strapped around corpulent middles, the grim click of loading mechanisms in the grey dawn—these things seem more like a prelude to battle than the beginning of a day's sport. There are whispered directions as groups plan a drive. All along the dirt roads through the scrub oak and pine and around the open fields of abandoned farms shadowy figures stand tense and watchful, hoping that some venturesome soul who has rashly entered the woods will jump a deer and put it out into the open. Somewhere off in the distance—not too far—a rifle spangs brassily and a self-dumper rips out its magazine contents as fast as the trigger can be pressed and released. The cold, frosty air fairly tingles and quivers with suspense and leashed fury as a hundred men snap off safeties or draw back hammers.

A few hundred yards back in the scrub a youth creeps slowly down an old game trail. He is quivering with eagerness and the hammer of his new 30-30 carbine is under his thumb, cocked and ready. The sun is not fully up, but it is light enough to see plainly and, just to be sure, he nervously throws the rifle to his shoulder and tries his vision on the sights.

The fact that his position in the thick brush ruins any chance he might have of seeing and getting a shot at a deer does not occur to him; he has a new rifle, is in the woods hunting, and this in itself is an exciting, thrilling experience. He knows nothing of woodcraft, has never seen a wild deer and has never even fired this new rifle that he appears to handle so deftly. He is the very greenest, most dangerous kind of a novice, but he is only one of hundreds thronging the woods this day. Peering, creeping, halting, he continues his fruitless stalk, until at last, tiring of the game, he pauses to rest and light a cigarette. The smoke is in his mouth and he is about to strike a match, when a dry twig snaps loudly a short distance off to his right. The cigarette, now entirely forgotten, dangles limply from his lip as he turns slowly, his mouth wide open in an effort to intensify his sense of hearing. There is another sound, a heavy, crunching step. The brush rustles and he sees a branch move not more than fifty feet away. His heart gives a leap and then thuds heavily as he stoops and peers through the dense cover. There is something standing there in the scrub, something big and alive and his excited brain creates a swift illusion of a head beneath branching antlers. He whips the rifle to his shoulder and at the shot there is a soft thud, a slight stirring in the dead leaves and all is quiet.

Wild-eyed he charges through the scrub to where his quarry lies. There is no breath, no life, no slightest movement in the man crumpled there in the dead leaves. His face is already turning grey from blood pumped furiously from the ragged hole in his neck and his eyes are turned up and locked in their sockets.

For a moment the youth stands literally frozen in his tracks with horror, and then terror and panic seize him. Turning from the dead man he runs wildly through the brush, leaping and scrambling over obstacles, bruising himself on trees and tearing his clothes on clinging branches until at last he comes into a road. After a time some measure of composure returns to him, and the man who gives him a ride into town suspects nothing.

He is safe, or so he thinks. Nobody has seen him near the man. The bullet plowing through the brush had mushroomed before it hit the man's neck, making a hole at the point of entrance nearly as large as fifty calibre, and then gone on through into the woods. The empty shell is still in the rifle, and he is snug at home.

Perhaps if he had gone back to the parked car and later joined the two friends he had started out with, things might have turned out differently, but running away from them and hitch-hiking home when they had planned to be out all day—well, the other boys wondered, they talked and the youth was picked up easily enough two days later. Nothing was ever done about it.

The Grand Jury thought he had suffered enough in his own mind so that further action was unnecessary, and perhaps that jury was right. It's not for me to judge.

The next year a father and son parked their car in that same scrub oak country. Neither of them knew anything about hunting, but their next-door neighbor had a deer hung up and had told them how easy it was to get one. The country was full of deer; anyone could shoot one who could point a gun and pull the trigger. So they rented two rifles, bought five cartridges for each, and set out confidently to kill two deer.

The father issued the strangest set of instructions that could be imagined. He said, "I'm going in here at the edge of this opening and make a half-circle. If you see or hear anything moving in there or see the bushes move, shoot and make sure you hit what you are shooting at." Those were his exact words according to the testimony of the boy at the investigation.

The man went into the brush, and having no knowledge of timing, direction or anything else, cut a very short circle and came to the edge of the clearing almost where he went in. The boy heard him coming, located him by sound and the moving brush and shot him just below the eyes with a 30-40 soft-nosed bullet. The man was killed instantly, and it didn't do the boy a whole lot of good either. Perhaps he would be better off with his father, considering the shape he is in mentally for one of those heavy soft-point bullets make an awful mess of a man's head.

Now, a review of all the hunting accidents I have investigated or helped investigate would fill quite a book and there is no point in going any further into the bloody details. These two are a couple of fair examples, and similar ones happen every year and evidently are going to keep right on happening as long as there are firearms in the hands of those who refuse to take them more seriously.

The clothing that hunters wear apparently has little to do with the prevention of accidents. Of course, if a man wants to go out and frolic around in something brown with a dash of white in it here and there, he will probably get it quicker than if he is draped in scarlet, but most of the men who are shot in the woods are wearing the conventional black and red checks. Bright crimson will no doubt bring a certain sense of security to its wearer, but even that will not stop a bullet.

I have always favored a black or navy blue jacket with a cap of the same material for travel in the brush during the deer season, but only last fall a sailor wearing his Navy pea jacket was shot out of an apple tree where he was watching for deer. The shooter in this case took him for a bear, so we can now cross off the black or blue clothing as a safety measure. There has been some agitation through various sporting periodicals for an examination of all prospective hunters before they may obtain a hunting license, but I fail to see how this would cut down these accidents. A man may know the mechanics of rifle shooting, he may be well versed in all kinds of woods lore gleaned from the pages of books and magazines, but there is surely something about the pursuit and subsequent slaying of moderately large warm-blooded animals that sets off some sort of an emotional disturbance that is entirely beyond any conventional course of training.

The numerous clubs and organizations affiliated with the National Rifle Association do an immense amount of good in teaching our American youth the correct way of handling firearms and familiarizing them with a weapon's potential deadliness, but what can be done to eliminate that temporary period of insanity that overtakes a man hell-bent on killing and temperamentally unfit for it? Some smart writer has suggested that every novice should go out into the woods and see deer in their natural habitat before being allowed to hunt them. That would be fine if one could find a country where deer were so thick during the hunting season that it would be possible to observe them at will, but right now I can't think of any such place.

What does a deer in the woods look like, anyway? I have seen them on the side of a ridge when they mingled with the mossy red of old pine stumps so perfectly that you couldn't tell the stumps from the deer without the aid of binoculars. When the hills turn steely grey in the fall the deer turn the same color around here, and through the screening growth of young beech saplings a deer is just a black nose, a pair of eyes and two ears. That is what you have to shoot at and nothing more or your buck may be a bobbing white tail dipping and soaring over blow-downs, or a grey shadow slipping through the tangle of a thicket. Some of them will stand around in an open field or an old orchard, but don't count on that. How a deer looks depends a good deal on its surroundings. I am quite positive that in different localities deer take on a decidedly different coloring, but probably there will be many naturalists who will not agree with me on that statement.

There is a wide gap between the conventional training that organizations and rifle clubs are able to give and the actual killing of game in the field. There are many shooters who could place their bullets anywhere on a cardboard silhouette of a deer, but would break and scatter lead all over the landscape if that inanimate object should suddenly come to life. How such human weaknesses can be overcome is a matter for future study, and I do not think any universal remedy will be found. We are all imbued with certain strong personal characteristics and mass instruction will hardly be effective in many individual cases.

There was a time when I thought satisfactory results might be obtained by offering aid and instruction to boys of grammar school age or a little younger, but I soon found out that the school children of today were not very receptive. Instead of attending school for the purpose of acquiring some small knowledge of useful subjects and a smattering of politeness and good conduct, they now enter their classrooms for the main purpose of cultivating their egos and flaunting their somewhat disgusting little personalities. Since their spirits are allowed to soar unfettered and they must be allowed full expression of their physical and mental impulses, they are so busily engaged in doing these things that any attempt at serious instruction or the application of mild discipline is apt to react unfavorably upon the instructor. A few of the boys who were interested in firearms and evidently had had some training at home showed a slight indication that they were grasping a few of the facts presented to them, but on the whole the children themselves or the grown-up male members of their families knew and forgot more about firearms and hunting accidents in one day than I could learn by careful observation in thirty years.

I remember overtaking a twelve-year-old on one of the back roads one day. He was wandering along carrying an old single-barreled shotgun over his shoulder, muzzle to the front. I glanced quickly at the breech and saw that the hammer was cocked, so I pulled up beside him and stopped the car.

I said pleasantly, "That's a very dangerous way to carry a gun. If you should stumble and fall the butt would come down on the ground hard and the muzzle would be right in your chest or stomach."

He stared at me insolently and snapped, "Any law against it?"

I answered that there was no law that I was supposed to enforce prohibiting him from shooting himself, but that there *was* a law against boys of his age hunting alone without a license. So he dropped the butt of the cocked gun roughly to the ground, hooked an arm around the barrel so that the muzzle rested under his left ear and produced a license. I checked it while he glared at me disdainfully, and then there was nothing else for me to do but drive away and leave him. I spoke to his father about the incident later in the day, and there was no doubt that he was the original block from whence came the chip. He suggested quite loudly and with profane emphasis that I quit pestering little kids and go out in the woods and arrest some of the lawbreakers of my own size. It was good advice and I took it.

It is the general practice among some of our native

hunters and guides to lay the blame for hunting accidents and the enormous loss of game through hasty and inaccurate shooting upon the shoulders of the so-called "sport," who is usually a hunter who does not reside in the State, or a resident who from the nature of his occupation is obliged to live in the city. From several years of personal observation, I will state flatly that this disposition of the case has now no basis in fact. There may have been a time when the sport looked kind of foolish, but right now most of them rate pretty high both as hunters and fishermen.

The city dweller who is sincerely interested in outdoor activities usually reads a lot and keeps himself well-informed on late developments in firearms. The chances are that he belongs to a rifle or pistol club and gets in a certain amount of shooting the year round. If he likes competitive shooting and is at all proficient in this sport, he has schooled his nerves and muscles to a point where they are under control, and before he takes his fall hunting trip he will take his rifle out to his local range and see that the sights are set for some predetermined range. When he reaches camp, he will try the rifle out again to be sure that the sights have not been moved in transit. He realizes from past experience or information that he has gained from reliable sources that he may obtain but one or two shots at a deer during his trip, and with this fact in mind he will try to make his first shot accurate and deadly.

I don't mean to say that this is true of *all* out-of-state or city hunters, since we gather in enough of them every year for buying deer to prove that a certain percentage visit us just for a good time and the actual hunting is apt to be quite sketchy. On the other hand, we gather in an equal number of residents for selling deer, so it comes out fairly even. Of course, there are a number in both categories who get away with this traffic, but we are hoping the day will come when the deer will be so plentiful that there will be no need of buying, and consequently, with the demand gone, there will be no more deer offered for sale.

I have talked with many resident hunters living near or in good deer country, who have seen and shot at from nine to twenty deer during the open season. Some of them hunt as long as the season lasts and do nothing else, and incredible as it may seem quite a few of them fail to hang up any meat. Around the village stores in the evenings there are long, bloody anecdotes told of deer knocked flat, blood, hair and bits of bone scattered around; and teeth, sections of jawbone or even a foreleg blown off the animal by an expanding bullet may be shown as proof of expert marksmanship and near-success.

After the season is closed and the snows have come, there will be fox trails leading to dozens of half-eaten carcasses, and worse still, the halting wavering tracks of the dying cripples. Some of them will have legs missing or dangling by the skin and cords, while others will be whole with the exception of their heads. They will have no upper or lower jawbones and will slowly starve. All this does not trouble the hunter, for the season is over and his mind will be on something else until November comes around again. Some of them will tell you frankly, "Hell, why should I spend a whole day trailing a few blood spots when the woods are full of deer and I can spend my time to better advantage looking for another deer?" Or, "This rifle, some way or other, shoots nearly two feet to the right and a foot low, an' half the time I forget. Held onto a doe's neck the other day an' damned if I didn't knock off a front leg! Held for the middle, so's to be sure the next shot an' knocked off a hind leg. Seems as if all this gun will do this year is shoot off legs."

Well, the remedy for that trouble should be plain enough, but although this man has shot at deer ever since he was big enough to carry a rifle, the simple adjustment of a set of sights is a mechanical mystery only to be intrusted to an expert gunsmith. "Can't lay a rifle up right in the middle of the season, but soon as it's over I'll have them cussed sights fixed."

One day during the early part of December, while cruising on foot in the town of Parsonfield, I came up wind into a hemlock run with a small brook running through it. The trees were quite large with very little underbrush among them and the air was damp and chilly with the promise of a cold rain. Halfway up the run I smelled something—a sour, disagreeable odor that I could not identify. It was not the smell of carrion, or any dead thing, and it reminded me strangely of a wound that I once had to dress several times a day—a wound that was feverish and would not heal right.

I quartered back and forth through the hemlocks, crossing the little brook several times, gaining and losing the scent, and then I came to a place where the brook widened into a little pool. On the opposite side of this pool from where I stood I could see a plain trail up the side of a slight incline and into a sparse thicket of young trees. I crossed the brook again to examine the trail and found that it had been in use for quite a few days. There was deer hair on it—white belly hair, scraping hoof marks and over it all a thin coating of slime and pale blood. I went up the trail a few steps toward the thicket. There was a sound of labored breathing and floundering and then the doe got painfully to her feet and stood there on three legs. She stood broadside to me, her head to my left and for a moment I could not grasp the significance of that great, red protrusion where her left hind leg and hip should have been. Her leg had been shot off at the thick part of the heavy bone just below the ham and the hide had peeled back leaving the whole hind quarter of red, living flesh exposed to the air. She trembled and sagged, even as I reached for my gun; and the 357 Magnum bullet that I put through her head was the kindest thing that ever happened to her.

A few days later I was describing this deer to a few interested listeners in one of the crossroads stores in an adjacent town, when one of my audience exclaimed, "Well, I'll be damned. I bet that's the same deer that I hit with my 300 Savage over to the foot of Province Lake. Took a runnin' shot at her an' she went end over end in a cloud of hair an' bone-splinters. Went down an' stayed down, an' then when I walked up to her, she up an' onto her feet and went into the timber with one leg a danglin' an' swingin' on the hamstring. Surprised me so when she come onto her feet ag'in that I never thought of givin' her the second one. Now who'd have thought you would have run onto that deer when it must have been as early as the twentieth of

November when I knocked that leg offen her! Boy, them deers is sure tough critters, ain't they?"

The answer is—yes, but not tough enough. They should have the teeth and claws of a lion and the hide and disposition of a rhinoceros—just to even things up a little.

CHAPTER XII

When I first saw the country around North Berwick, Sanford and North Shapleigh, I had a good mind to turn in my badge and go home. The possibility that any decent amount of game could use those pine and scrub oak plains for cover seemed slim, and the lack of cedar for winter browse condemned the area on sight, because I knew, or thought I knew, that deer could not survive severe winters without cedar. This had been told to me often enough by people who were woods-wise, and I was openly skeptical of the district's ability to produce any great amount of game. But there were deer all through that scrub and, when the snow left in the spring, it was not at all unusual to see eight or ten in a bunch leisurely crossing the macadam roads.

Just before I took over the district there were over a hundred deer yarded in one small basin at the foot of Abbot Mountain in the town of Shapleigh, and people went in there Sundays on snowshoes to take pictures of them. I kept hearing about deer and still more deer, and then I began to locate them myself, scattered all through the plains, bunched on the sunny slopes and standing around in the open fields. One could drive out after dark almost any night and pick up a dozen pairs of eyes through the clover patches and back roads, and jacking was rampant. We soon ganged up on the jackers and thinned them out while the number of deer grew steadily larger.

After the first snow, the roads and fields around Newfield and North Shapleigh would be a maze of tracks. Sign was so fresh and so thick that it was impossible to pick out any one deer and trail it. The deer went from these open places down across Giles Plains and into a series of deep runs filled with scrub oak and grey birch. In that tangle of dense thickets they were invisible at a distance of fifty feet, and there were few hunters hardy enough to attempt to move them out. It couldn't be done, anyway, for when they were jumped, they simply made a short half circle, or ducked over a ridge and into another deep gully.

In a game country slashed and crisscrossed with dozens of roads, rough but passable for automobiles, there is bound to be a certain amount of illegal killing, especially during the late summer and early fall, but after a two-year period of fast and constant activity, we cleaned up most of the professional bad boys, and I found that my greatest trouble was to come from dogs.

This business of dogs killing deer is something that most wardens find very unpleasant to deal with, especially if they happen to like dogs. Despite a very rigid law which states that an officer may kill any dog that is found in the act of chasing deer, a great many dog-owners profess to be ignorant of it. In fact, I found that telling a man he has a deer-killing dog is about like informing a New England housewife that there are bedbugs in her home. You can tell some men that their wives are stepping out, that their daughters are not behaving as they should, and they will take the information with a measure of equanimity; but when you inform them that their dogs have been running deer, just anchor yourself firmly and prepare to ride out a big wind. The storm will eventually blow over, but the chances are that the dog will keep right on running until stopped by a slug.

Now almost any kind of a dog will run deer, but it is only the confirmed killer that shows obvious signs of guilt. I have picked up dozens of spaniels, beagles and even fox and 'coon hounds, put them in my car and brought them to their owners. They came upon deer unexpectedly, found it fun to give them a run and then got lost. When you speak to a dog alone out on the highway and he acts friendly, it is a pretty good indication that he has no real criminal record; and, strange as it may seem, the habitual deer killer will usually drop his tail and run the minute a warden tries to approach. I have checked closely a great many times and feel quite certain that the dog knows it is doing wrong and feels a sense of guilt.

Although some attempt has been made to compile records concerning the number of deer killed by dogs during a certain period, no accurate estimate can be made because a great many deer are lost after the snow has melted. When the lush vegetation of late May and June blooms, visual signs are almost nonexistent, and the discovery of carcasses will be mostly by accident. I believe, however, that the loss from dogs alone will exceed the kill from both bobcats and poachers during a calendar year, throughout the entire State, and I do not feel that this phase of conservation has in the past received the attention that it should.

The killing of a few deer by bobcats is always a news item welcomed by the press and sporting magazines, and the arrest and conviction of any individual connected with an illegal killing is often given space on the front page, but this constant and serious loss of our finest game animal through the depredation of household pets is passed over lightly or entirely ignored.

During the fall and early winter the deer can take care of themselves, but from the middle of March on into June, when the does are heavy and the bucks sluggish from the drain of the long winter, the big mongrels, German Shepherds and this breed crossed with hounds will make bloody inroads upon the deer herds. A hunting hound will trail a deer all day, making a lot of noise and doing little damage, but these big German Shepherds and their crosses, trained down to bone and sinew, running fast and silently and often in pairs or trios, will leap at a deer's hind legs, throw it and in a fury of slashing teeth and flying deer hair tear open the hams and rip out the intestines while the struggling, blatting victim flounders frantically around, covering the snow with hair and blood. It is a horribly slow and painful death because in most cases the dogs confine their attack to the rear of the animal, leaving the heart and lungs to function until the end comes from sheer terror, pain, and exhaustion. I once saw an area, which could be enclosed in a circle of fifty yards in diameter, trampled, blood-splashed and covered with deer hair, showing plainly just how desperate the struggle had been. A few days later, when two dogs that were making the most of a firm crust put another deer out onto the ice of the river, less than a hundred yards from where I stood watching the crossing place, the sharp jolt of my old Springfield Sporter felt good to my shoulder, and the two killers flattened into two dark smudges upon the gleaming ice.

The first year I hardly made a dent in the dog population. After the second year of shooting, serving notices and making myself very disagreeable indeed, I found that the dog-owners were keeping their dogs home during the day and letting them run at night. So I perfected a method of close-range night shooting and worked on the proposition day and night. During eight years of constant effort, I know I made some progress, and the people in my district finally admitted that the steadily increasing number of deer registered during open season was owing in great part to my war on the dogs. I shot none but the actual deer chasers and, although there was a certain amount of unpleasantness, I tried to be fair and treat all alike. It made no difference who owned the dog or how much it was worth; if it killed deer and I could find it behind one, it died and that was all there was to it.

There was trouble—plenty of it—but for every enemy I made, I acquired a hundred friends, and after a time the actual killing decreased. The deer lingered tamely around the villages during the summer, and there was decided improvement all around. But I couldn't stop the business completely. Every year a new pack of killers, fast, silent and deadly, would show up in the district to leave a trail of torn carcasses on the runways.

During the spring of 1944 I hunted for six weeks a

pack of three dogs that killed four deer the first week in March. I saw them on the State highway twice, but since they were not actually in pursuit of deer, I could do nothing. Nobody would admit ownership and I could get no information about where they came from. They were as wild as wolves, and the second my car stopped they were off the road and into the woods.

Finally, I caught them in the open, close behind a wheezing, limping doe. They saw me at the same instant I saw them and, leaving the deer, they wheeled and went down an old rocky dirt road. One went flat at the first shot, a second rolled end over end as a bullet smashed a rock to splinters just under his belly, and the third slipped into the brush before I could get another shell into the chamber. The dog with the rock-splinters in his hide rolled into the ditch and got away too, so I got only one out of the pack, but that one was enough. The other two left that part of the country and were never seen again.

Most people wait until all chance of effective action is over before they make a complaint, and even then they won't give a good description of a dog; or tell who owns it. But once in a while some good citizen will rise up in honest wrath and save a warden a lot of travel and worry.

When my telephone rang at seven o'clock on that morning of April 4, 1944, it didn't seem as if I could possibly get out of bed. I had been watching a smelt brook until two a.m., and when I had finally got to bed my throat and ears ached so that sleep was impossible without medical aid. I was a sick man—a lot sicker than

I knew—but I took a couple of pills and finally passed out.

My wife took the phone message. She said, "A man over toward Limington called and said two dogs just drove a deer through his pasture and were quite close to it. He says, if you go by the gravel pit to Clark Brook, they should cross the open meadow in a few minutes. He will get in his car and meet you on the road."

Fumbling and groaning, my head fuzzy and numb, I got into some clothes, shoved my feet into a pair of rubber boots and stumbled out to my car. It was a cold, grey morning with a hint of snow in the air and, as I turned off on a side road as directed, I wished that I had waited for a cup of hot coffee. I came out into the open fields beyond the gravel pit and there was a man standing in the middle of the road. He was very old and very excited, and he was also very angry—profanely so. He waved his cane toward the meadows off to my right. "There they be, goddam um, there they be, an' how in hell be ye goin' to get to um?"

Nearly three hundred yards out across the partially flooded meadow two dogs were tearing savagely at the hindquarters of a big doe. She was alive and struggling, and even as I reached for my rifle, she got her front legs under her and raised her forequarters from the ground. One of the dogs, a big smooth-haired mongrel, nearly all black, left her rear and leaped at her head just as I slid home a clip of shells and closed the bolt. One doesn't see the actual killing very often. You find the mangled remains, see the dogs behind the deer and sometimes at the dead body, but the business going on out there on the snow was something I had witnessed only once before and the whole scene seemed to take on a peculiar dreamlike quality.

The old man's squalling did not bother me. He squealed, "Hell an' damnation, you can't hit northin' from here, you'll jest scare um off."

The black dog's jaws closed over the doe's nose. He pulled her head down, braced his feet and wrenched her head and neck savagely, turning and twisting it. The ivory bead on my front sight came up from below, touched the tense, straining black body, crept a little higher and then it seemed as if, through no volition of my own, the rifle muzzle leaped and the dog was a flat, dark blot on the grey snow. The doe stretched her neck straight out and lay quiet.

I worked the bolt and chambered another shell. The other dog stopped his gnawing and turned his head toward me and then, as I tried to put the bead on him, I realized that he was nearly all white. The ivory bead and the white dog against the snow—it was like shooting at a wisp of fog. I let go and missed. The dog ran over to the dead one, sniffed at the body and, as he raised his head, I missed again. He turned and walked slowly toward the alders at the edge of the meadow and I wasted my third shot at him. It went over, like the others.

If I had been in full possession of my faculties, I would probably have fired the last cartridge in my rifle hurriedly and lost him, but I took plenty of time in this half-trance I seemed to be in. Just as the white dog reached the dense thicket of small alders, he turned and looked back at the deer. For a few seconds I had a white dog against a dark background. I put the bead over him on the dark smudge of the thicket and let it slowly down while I took up the slack in the trigger. That shot wasn't fifty percent luck or ninety-nine percent. It was *all* luck.

"Boy," said the old man solemnly, "I heered you was a patient son-of-a-bitch with a rifle, but keep a-tryin' to reach out that way an' you're going to strain that bar'l."

That illness I went through turned out to be quite serious. I spent a lot of money on treatments for strep throat and nearly died twice during the winter of 1944. But when it began to look like spring and the snow was shrinking fast, I improved considerably and took a notion to write this book. It took me longer than I had hoped, for my health is still not good, and now it is another spring—1946—as I finish.

The day before yesterday I went down and opened up my little cabin, built up a fire and wrote steadily for at least four hours. My camp is high above the cove where my grandfather made his play for those geese, and today I counted fifty-four fat Canadas just within rifle range out in front of the old blind. There haven't been that many geese since I was a boy in school and I take it as a good omen.